TOP TIER LEADERSHIP

A Thirty Day Leadership Journey

ROB MANNING

WESTBOW
PRESS®
A DIVISION OF THOMAS NELSON
& ZONDERVAN

Copyright © 2020 Rob Manning.

All rights reserved. No part of this book may be used or reproduced by any means, graphic, electronic, or mechanical, including photocopying, recording, taping or by any information storage retrieval system without the written permission of the author except in the case of brief quotations embodied in critical articles and reviews.

This book is a work of non-fiction. Unless otherwise noted, the author and the publisher make no explicit guarantees as to the accuracy of the information contained in this book and in some cases, names of people and places have been altered to protect their privacy.

WestBow Press books may be ordered through booksellers or by contacting:

WestBow Press
A Division of Thomas Nelson & Zondervan
1663 Liberty Drive
Bloomington, IN 47403
www.westbowpress.com
1 (866) 928-1240

Because of the dynamic nature of the Internet, any web addresses or links contained in this book may have changed since publication and may no longer be valid. The views expressed in this work are solely those of the author and do not necessarily reflect the views of the publisher, and the publisher hereby disclaims any responsibility for them.

Any people depicted in stock imagery provided by Getty Images are models, and such images are being used for illustrative purposes only.
Certain stock imagery © Getty Images.

ISBN: 978-1-9736-8265-3 (sc)
ISBN: 978-1-9736-8267-7 (hc)
ISBN: 978-1-9736-8266-0 (e)

Library of Congress Control Number: 2019920841

Print information available on the last page.

WestBow Press rev. date: 02/14/2020

This book reflects a life lived with remarkable people. None more remarkable than my wife, my love, my best friend Susan. She tolerated fourteen houses and thirteen different jobs with patience, kindness, and support. She pushed her own loved career to the back and rallied behind my own. Throughout more than forty years together, she has grown to become my picture of Philippians 1:21, "For me, to live is Christ." I see Christ in her every day. Her humility and devotion, her love and support, and her perseverance and patience reflect the Christ who lives within her. She is my hero, my model for true leadership, and she has shaped any success I may have had through the years.

"They who wait for the Lord shall renew their strength; they shall mount up with wings like eagles; they shall run and not be weary; they shall walk and not faint."[1]

---

[1] Isaiah 40:31

In the Beginning

Nothing screams lazy like a twelve-year-old on summer break. The whole summer lay before me there in the little community called Farm Life. I had everything planned. Sleep first, eat, head to the pool, then sleep some more before eating again. The summer of 1968 was going to be the best summer ever. Yet it only took a few moments to all come crashing down. My mom flicked on my bedroom light and said, "Get on your work clothes. You've got a job!" Within an hour I was in the tobacco field. This is how my first day working for real money began. It was time for the twelve-year-old to learn what it means to work. That twelfth year was to be a hard summer. But one of my best summers ever, just as I planned. Bonding with other kids my age and with men and women—all with a single, simple mission: Get the tobacco in the barn before nightfall. Working side-by-side, age making no difference.

Just after dawn, when the dew was settling on the gummy, green leaves, I was ready to make money at my first real job—driving the tractor that pulled the tobacco harvester through the fields. I crawled up onto the tractor and cranked the diesel engine. Even at twelve years old I had been driving tractors for years. I turned to watch as men and women climbed onto the harvester, even as I steered the tractor down the rows, harvester in tow, barely above a snail's pace.

The tobacco field was set up in rows to accommodate the wide, awkward harvester. The field began with four rows aligned closely together, like our garden at home. Then came a wide middle row, called creatively, *the middle*. Then four more closely spaced rows, followed by another middle. I could see that this pattern continued for acres and acres. I was driving my tractor down *the middle*. This allowed people working in workstations mounted on the harvester's main structure to have direct access to the row directly on either side of *the middle*.

Swinging from an extendable arm stretching out over the top of the tobacco plants was still another workstation, one on each side of the harvester. These swinging workstations worked the next rows over from my tractor, beyond those rows directly beside me. In this way, the harvester worked two rows on each side of *the middle*. We worked four rows total, with four workstations and one brand new tractor driver whose job was to just keep the harvester in the *middle*.

Each of the four workstations held two seated workers, a primer and a looper. Tobacco pickers or *primers*, normally men, sat at the back of each workstation, riding through the fields facing forward toward my tractor. The primers sat in a seat mounted near the level of the lowest tobacco leaf, just above the ground. One by one, the primers picked the bottom, yellowing, ripe leaves, called "priming tobacco." I was told that priming was the most difficult work, done only by the most experienced workers. Priming was hard, fast, repetitive, dirty work. As the primers picked tobacco with one hand, they passed leaves up with the other hand to the skill position, the "loopers."

Loopers, normally women, sat in the workstation facing their primer, looking backwards on the harvester, away from my tractor. Loopers sat in permanently mounted seats welded about three feet higher than the primers. From my front-row tractor seat I could turn to watch as the tobacco harvester rolled slowly through the field, reaching across those four rows of tobacco. On each row, a primer and a looper worked together to produce sticks of green tobacco. The primers handed up leaves as they picked them, in groups of three-or-four leaves at a time. Loopers wrapped string around the leaves and strapped them to tobacco sticks. First one side, then flipping over to the other side of the stick.

Riding center on the back of the harvester was the lone standing man, my Uncle Zack, who was always the lead man when I was working on his farm. As one of the four loopers yelled "Stick!" my uncle grappled the stick full of yellow-green leaves away from the looper and stacked the tobacco-laden stick on a pallet trailing the harvester down the row.

Uncle Zack controlled the speed, yelling "Up!" for more speed or "Slow!" when the ripe leaves began to overpower the primers who were picking the tobacco. He often gauged this process by the amount of conversation between the men and women on the harvester. I learned to anticipate his call and inch the tractor throttle up and down.

As the day progressed, we even tried out our voices at singing together. All the families I worked with were church people, so we naturally sang church songs. My uncle sang in a gospel quartet, so we sang a lot of gospel music on the harvester, that is until my uncle would tire of singing or realize it was time to pick up the pace. He'd yell, "Up!" and I'd knock the throttle up a notch. Then the conversation or singing was quickly replaced with a sole focus on our work. At the end of the day, all the men and women were covered in the gum of tobacco.

Driving the tractor through the field was my first job, a position for the least experienced, the kids. The only skill required was keeping the tractor in the center of the row as it dragged the harvester. A few times, I found myself nodding off from boredom. The tractor would slowly inch out of the lane, pulling the harvester behind. This would get a quick reprimand from Uncle Zack, "Stay awake up there!" Foot by foot the harvester crew danced through the field, each person doing his or her part.

Finally, when the row ended, the harvester crew would step off for a quick break as the hanging crew loaded the full pallet onto another tractor and headed off to hang the sticks in the old, flu-curing barn. Here at the end of each row came my greatest challenge as the new kid, tractor driver. Here I needed to clear the row carefully so I could steer the whole tractor/harvester contraption into the adjacent rows. It took a little practice, but I was soon as good as anyone. As the harvester entered another group of four rows, the dance began anew. Before long, the drudgery of work faded as the pleasure of friendship overpowered the toil.

True lasting friendship rose from our constant verbal exchange as our work just went on and on. In time I advanced beyond tractor driver to real work, hanging the full sticks in the barn. Hanging was a job for teenagers. This required tremendous dexterity and almost unlimited energy. Hanging was a tough job, but easy enough to master. Hanging also pointed toward the ultimate job of primer. Priming was the pinnacle job, the hardest job and the most well paid.

In the depths of these never-ending fields I learned to respect my mother's side of the family. Here I saw the strength, love, and dignity of my Uncle Zack and cousins Zack Jr. and Bill. They were passionate, raw and intense people, with tempers and faults that were overcome by an extraordinary love for farming and an extraordinary love for each other, which had been fettered by the real power of the family, my Aunt Loreta (pronounced LorEEta).

For the first time in my life I was learning skills and trading those skills for real cash. The tobacco summers were my first chance to pick up the mantel of work. Fifty years later I would finally lay that mantel down again. Many of the lessons I learned that summer long ago remained as building blocks in the stack that continued to grow block-by-experiential block as I worked over the next fifty years.

Those early years solidified a work ethic in me. This work ethic was common enough among the hard-working farmers of the Farm Life community, but surprisingly different from the halls of corporate offices. What was commonplace in the fields proved to be extraordinarily valuable in Duke Power Company's High Point, North Carolina, office when I was a naïve young engineer.

Duke Power, later Duke Energy, was kind to my family and me. For thirty years I learned the craft of keeping the lights burning as we bounced our family from town to town. It would be twenty-two years before my first vice president's job. In the following eight years, I would hold four more vice-president titles. My last Duke Energy job was my favorite at Duke, VP of Field Operations, Carolinas. What a great title, almost like being back in the tobacco field again. Except this time our job was making sure people in the Carolinas had the luxury of electricity at their fingertips anytime, all the time. I owe much to Duke. Perhaps more than anything else, they taught me the craft of leadership.

After thirty years I left Duke for the Tennessee Valley Authority (TVA). This was a big move from one of the preeminent "for-profit" enterprises to the largest public power utility in the United States. I took the role of Executive Vice President of Power System Operations. Another fantastic title. I never had so much fun working in all my life. The idea of public power was new to me. Public Power is designed to be owned by the people served. There is no focus on profit or loss. The focus is on cost and service. This different idea of delivering electricity to people exploded all around me. It was a wonderful experience working with wonderful people.

But leading in public power was also hard work. Stripped bare of my familiar Duke Energy underpinnings, TVA gave me the first real chance to be *the* leader. Duke possessed a broad and effective support system for leaders, people who propped you up and kept you moving forward despite yourself. Lean TVA had no such support system. As a leader, you were the whole package, little help was coming your way. This was both fulfilling and humbling. I worked at TVA for six years before shifting once more. I finished my career doing research work, joining the Electric Power Research Institute (EPRI) as the Vice President of Transmission and Distribution.

My work life has been an amazing journey of success and failures. Of highs and lows. Throughout this journey my wife and family continued to provide tremendous support and blessings. I have served outstanding leaders. I have had many remarkable experiences. Family, leaders, and experiences taught me many lessons. Over the years, God weighed in as well. Like anyone, I went through times when my work defined me. My success at work meant I was a success in life. My failures at work felt like failures in life. *But God . . .*

Some of my favorite parts of the Bible begin with "But God." This beautiful phrase often follows the worst of times. The battle seems to be over. But then God shows up and everything changes. I can't point exactly to my first "But God" moment, but I believe it started at TVA. I was commuting, living apart from my wife for the first time, and working lots of hours. I was traveling home over the weekends and continuing to teach Sunday school at church. Somehow sitting all alone at night in Chattanooga, Tennessee, the words of the Bible began to jump off the page. I had read the Bible for years but never had I *felt* the Bible. Those long lonely evenings became simply extended quiet times with God. Here I was leading hundreds of people, but what was I doing for the Lord? I thought I was there for work, but it turned out the work was there for me, a conduit so I could become a better Christian and a better leader.

This is where life gets difficult. Most of the world defines a bright line of separation between church and state. This means your religion is likely not welcome in the corporate office. Many companies have definitive, strong policies that limit religious activity. As leaders, our company expects us to follow the policies set before us. How then can we demonstrate our

Christianity and at the same time toe the line of policy? In fact, I remember praying this prayer, *Lord, what can I do about this situation when it conflicts with what I feel is the right decision? It's against the rules. In some cases, it's against the law!* I could almost hear the Lord chuckling to that one. "*Do not think that I have come to abolish the Law or the Prophets; I have not come to abolish them but to fulfill them.*"[2]

Turns out Christians can navigate the complexities of law and policy and also be successful! People recognize Christians by their actions, their lifestyles, their choices. What greater law than to love one another? What greater policy than respect for all? But it is not easy to always make the right choice, to live the right way, and to find joy along the way.

Early at TVA, a group of line workers asked me what my leadership philosophy was. I had to think on that question. For years at Duke I always told people to simply, "Do the right thing. No matter what, always do the right thing." This can be harder than it sounds, for understanding the right thing is quite a challenge. On that day at TVA, I added a second idea, "Know what the right thing is." Then I remembered my time in the tobacco fields and added, "Always have fun at your job." These three ideas resonated in their simplicity. They became my three leadership imperatives. From these imperatives grew my walk as both a Christian and a leader.

For the remainder of our time together, I would like to share my experiences and the experiences of others as we fought to follow these imperatives. After introducing each imperative a number of attributes will follow. These attributes are core, foundational skills, which add up to leadership consistency within the imperative. As you layer in these skills, your Christian pathway begins to mark the route within the complicated policy path of business. In time, the way becomes clearer, easier.

We will also look at what God's Word, the Holy Bible, has to say about each particular aspect of leadership. As you work through each lesson God has for you, pray for guidance, for wisdom, for effective application of the lessons He teaches you through His Word. I encourage you to walk through day by day. Sit with each attribute, particularly those where you need personal growth. Pray over its application to your own life and leadership. And watch to see how God highlights leadership qualities in the people around you.

---

[2] Matthew 5:*17*

Embrace God's Word, embrace your fundamental beliefs, and let your faith guide your leadership. Faith-based leadership doesn't have to be contrary to your company's expectations. In fact, faith-based leadership is sound leadership in any and every environment.

God is ready to bless you, to use you for His purpose. If you are striving for a position of leadership, you don't need to compromise your Christianity to be successful. If you are already a leader, God can use your Christianity to grow your leadership *and* your influence. You *can* be a successful leader *and* live for Christ. I wish you great success in both. Thank you for considering the leadership challenges in this book.

DAY ONE
The First Imperative: Do the Right Thing

Biblical Reference: James 4:17

> *"So whoever knows the right thing to do and fails to do it, for him it is sin."*

A few years ago, TVA became one of the last public corporations to outlaw public prayer. This became a highly volatile issue, since at the time many meetings opened in prayer. As a leader, the choice is complex. Do you violate company policy and hold open prayer? Or do you risk violating a biblical principle by no longer praying? Doing the right thing is complicated. In this case, the focus changed to a time for private prayer rather than open, communal prayer. This approach, while not ideal for a room full of like-minded believers, leaves the door open for biblical prayer without overtly violating a corporate rule. This compromise preserved the power of prayer in the workplace while satisfying the clear direction of company policy.

The first imperative comes straight from Psalm 119.[3] As leaders, we must "Do the Right Thing." This sounds simple but can be so complex. Is the right thing defined by your corporation, as in TVA's prayer policy? Is the right thing defined by your circumstances? At TVA I conducted meetings every day. Some meetings were small, just a few people, and some

---

[3] Psalm 119:105-106 *"Your word is a lamp to my feet and a light to my path. I have sworn an oath and confirmed it, to keep your righteous rules."*

were hundreds of people. Normally the large events held opening prayer to begin the meeting. Communal prayer was the accepted thing to do. It felt like the right thing to do. Yet people opposed to prayer were sitting among us, and the policy clearly stated no open, communal prayer.

When we switched to a moment of silence and reflection, some of us were uncomfortable at first. Some people didn't like the change. However, when balanced against the alternative of eliminating prayer altogether, people grew comfortable with private prayer, and we met the company policy. These types of decisions are complicated, how do we know what is right? At TVA the compromise of private prayer met both the requirement of company policy and the need to honor God in opening prayer through our private reflections. But was private prayer the right thing to do? Maybe the right thing is the uncompromising support of biblical principles in all situations? Or maybe the right thing is to find a compromise.

The answer to all these questions is "Yes." When you are working for a corporation, the corporation sets the foundational practices required for employees, particularly for leaders. Most of these company policies are not likely to be in direct conflict with biblical principles. Likewise, circumstances may shift the compass needle around depending on where, when, and how one is engaged with others. TVA decided to comply with state and federal law and eliminate open prayer before meetings, for example. Of course, biblical principles provide the foundation for all decisions, and compromising biblical principles is a pathway to ruin (see verse eight of Psalm 1.)[4]

The change in the prayer policy at TVA is a simple example of a complex problem, merging Christianity and corporate policy. This problem requires more of us as Christian leaders who must work inside the worldly system to be the best leader possible—while at the same time keeping the light of God shining. The world knows how to build good leaders. The body of Christ knows how to shape men and women into servant leaders who seek the will of God. A select few leaders find a way to balance both.

The most important part of leading is not toggling through the mental checklist of leadership requirements, casting a vision and mission statement, or acting strategically, or communicating with passion. These

---

[4] Psalm 1:8 *"For the Lord watches over the way of the righteous, but the way of the wicked leads to ruin."*

kinds of leadership requirements are great within themselves, but checking them off like checking a grocery list dooms us to mediocrity. The checklist approach appears autocratic and unprepared. To lead, you must know the way. Knowing the way means *knowing* the way, not referencing your checklist. People follow because they trust you, and people trust those who know the way. At Duke Power I became so experienced with leading storm recovery that I inherently knew the way. I didn't need manuals or instructions, because the approach to successful power restoration lived within my experiences and was always readily available for action. I knew the way, because I had been that way many times before.

To know the way, leadership principles are internalized, a part of you. God uses this same approach with Scripture; Psalm 119 advises that you should hide these words in your heart.[5] The words of Scripture are internal. You don't have to go look up something in the Bible when faced with an immediate decision to sin or not sin. Led by the Spirit and directed by the words of the Bible hidden within your heart, you already know the right thing to do. This is also true as a leader.

In fact, leadership success flows out of competent consistency. Competent consistency demands intentionality, and intentionality comes from a well-defined pathway born from years of example and experience. This pathway echoes the words I shared years ago with that group of linemen. Do the right thing. Know the right thing to do. Find joy in all you do.

Circumstances make right and wrong complicated. Consider the issue faced regularly by electric line workers. One of my first leadership actions involved a controversy around grounding lines. Duke Power Company policy states clearly that *all* wires require bonding electrically to the ground itself. In this particular situation, my line workers drove up on a car accident and wires were down all around and on top of the car. They never doubted the line was de-energized, because they came directly from the substation to the wreck. Yet policy is clear, do not move the lines until grounded. However, the line workers determined that grounding these wires would be more dangerous than donning rubber protective gloves and moving the lines away from traffic before beginning their work. It

---

[5] Psalm 119:11 *"I have stored up your word in my heart, that I might not sin against you."*

was a gray area. The policy was clear, but in practice, the policy required an application of knowledge and experience.

Nine times out of ten, maybe ninety times out of one hundred, the policy is correct. But in this situation, the line workers based their decision on their experience and their regard for their own safety. Another supervisor noticed that these workers had not followed policy and reported them. In the end, I had to respect their judgment and agree with their decision. Line workers understand that this policy is not always going to fit every circumstance, so these workers used their experience and knowledge to apply policy correctly. They were prepared for their decision through years of experience.

We cannot internalize the right thing without preparation. It is not enough to know company policy. We must also understand why the policy exists. Just as electric linemen apply knowledge of policy in specific circumstances, we must see right clearly within all circumstances. It is not enough to be able to quote Bible verses, we must understand the intent, context, and focus of the verse and be able to apply that verse rapidly to unfolding situations. Only with sufficient biblical foundation can we consistently do the right thing.

Consider each of the attributes that follow: integrity, confidence, boldness, action, a tough yet gentle approach, presence, and perseverance. These attributes fine tune our ability to do the right thing as outlined by James 4:17, *"So whoever knows the right thing to do and fails to do it, for him it is sin."* As we layer in these skills, we build understanding and context for doing the right thing. We also learn how to take our individual gifts as Christians and stand our ground, even as those around us waiver.

Today, pause and pray that you might be open to the Lord's teaching.

Pray that the words on these pages serve as guides that reveal the Spirit's direction for your character. Pray that opportunities present themselves that you might demonstrate and remember the things you learn. Pray for your leaders, pray for your followers, pray for yourself, that you might fully align with God's plan. Finally, thank God for your opportunities and praise Him for His leadership in your life.

DAY TWO
The First Imperative: Do the Right Thing

INTEGRITY

> *"Integrity is the ability to hold onto a consistent moral direction. It is the willingness to decide rightly no matter the consequences of the decision."*[6]

Biblical Reference: Proverbs 11:3

> *"The integrity of the upright guides them, but the crookedness of the treacherous destroys them."*

In the later years of my career, I had the pleasure of traveling to Japan and South Korea for business. Both the Japanese and South Koreans are wonderful people and truly interested in expanding their knowledge of other cultures. Both the Japanese and South Koreans have an enormous work ethic that results in high productivity and great business results. This ethic also results in long working hours, time away from home, and a focus on delivering results that borders on unhealthy. The South Korean custom is for businessmen and women to gather after work daily for drinks. Often these barroom meetings result in significant business deals. This custom builds camaraderie and bonds the team. However, this custom also fractures families by extending already long workdays. This deeply

---

[6] https://en.wikipedia.org/wiki/Integrity

embedded cultural expectation is clear for any business person visiting. You join the after-hours sessions and participate. Many international deals come from barroom discussions rather than boardrooms.

I serve as a deacon at my church. This is a time-honored position of leadership and service and comes with many requirements. While not true at many churches, my church asks deacons to abstain from alcohol while on active deacon service. You may disagree with my church's philosophy of abstinence for deacons or elders. But our jot-and-tittle theology is not the issue. The point is, I agreed to abstain when I agreed to serve. No matter your interpretation of biblical guidance for alcohol use, I signed an agreement that said I would not use alcohol. Once I signed the agreement, drinking became an integrity issue. To sign means to accept the terms. To sign and not accept the terms is a failure of integrity.

As a visitor, I often joined the South Koreans after work. As the team continued to celebrate drink after drink, I nursed my Diet Coke, often until early morning hours. Time after time, this confounded my South Korean friends, who simply could not fathom the idea of not drinking alcohol. Yet, over time, my new friends would come and tell me (usually the next day) how much they respected my living up to a commitment. Time after time, abstinence gave me an opportunity to share my faith. While I may have cemented fewer deals in the evenings than my peers, the South Koreans clearly trusted my integrity as I worked with them throughout the daylight hours. Perhaps this paid higher dividends over the long term than the barroom junkets.

We cannot hope to consistently do the right thing without integrity as a firm foundation. Integrity is the applied sum of life experience and knowledge. Integrity grows as we grow. At a young age we all struggle to accept the consequences of our decisions. But, as we grow, our character forms as layers of experience and knowledge shape how we respond to issues and challenges. The more we demonstrate integrity, the more internalized our integrity response becomes. And the more knowledge we have of the circumstances around us, the more likely we are to make good decisions.

Unfortunately, leadership can open doorways to tempt those willing to trade integrity for anything else (results, money, power, recognition). I had a boss who was rumored to be embezzling funds. Even before the rumor was fully investigated, no one would ever follow him again as he had clearly demonstrated he was not worthy of trust. Followers greatly value the predictability and consistency that comes from integrity, even at the expense of results or money or power. Most followers appreciate a leader whose consistent moral compass outweighs the short-term potential of sacrificing the right thing for immediate gain.

Integrity requires a lifetime of commitment. A single missed step can easily lead to another and another one, which will ultimately lead to an integrity crisis. Consider the parade of men who exposed their weak moral compasses. CEO's who lost their position because of improper infidelity or illegal actions. Or the historical fall of public church leaders who lose their way. Integrity is hard, very hard. Standing your moral ground will sometimes cost you popularity, but you will gain respect. And people follow those they respect.

Integrity is always the first step to leadership. Perhaps you have integrity in abundance. Perhaps you have integrity, but a momentary slip leaves you seeking to recover. Perhaps you find yourself embedded in a culture that values financial results over everything, including integrity. It does not matter where you have been, so much as where you seek to go. Today is the first day to embrace a life of integrity. Like my South Korean visits, you may sacrifice moments of success, but reap dividends throughout your life.

Ask yourself these questions:

- Am I comfortable in my moral foundation?
- Do I regularly and consistently demonstrate integrity?
- Do I yield to the temptation of compromise? What can I do to address these temptations?

Today, pray for integrity.

Pray that the Holy Spirit will write a moral compass upon your heart that alerts you to potential compromise. Pray Proverbs 11:3, that the integrity of the upright might guide you. Confess your shortfalls and pray for improvement. Pray for your leaders to have integrity, pray for your followers to have integrity. Pray God will present you with an opportunity to demonstrate integrity. Pray that the Holy Spirit gives you the power to overcome challenges to your personal integrity. Finally, thank God for your opportunities and praise Him for His leadership in your life.

DAY THREE
The First Imperative: Do the Right Thing

CONFIDENCE

"Confidence is a feeling of trust and firm belief in yourself or others."[7]

Biblical Reference: Proverbs 3:26

"For the Lord will be your confidence and will keep your foot from being caught."

Many years ago, an opportunity occurred for me to serve as "supervisor on call" for the first time. The call came about 2 A.M. and with it came my first chance to shine. An early morning wreck had clipped a power pole about a half hour away. When I drove up, the scene was chaotic. Telephone and power lines were draped over the car. Firemen stood there, wary of the potential hazard. I confirmed it was safe to remove the car from under the lines and within minutes the ambulance and tow truck cleared the street. Now I found myself alone and the damage was obvious. The power pole was completely severed. The bottom of the pole sat on the ground, pushed to the side almost a foot.

Looking up, I saw that this was a critical power pole, a four-way intersection of important circuits. Moving quickly, I made a radio call to

---

[7] https://www.vocabulary.com/dictionary/confidence

North State Telephone Company, who owned the pole. Duke and North State split pole ownership in High Point and paid rental fees to use each other's poles. I requested a new forty-foot pole as soon as possible. Next, I needed to get the linemen. I asked dispatch to pull them out of bed, instruct them to pick up a line truck, and meet me at the office to gather materials. Everything was going well, and my confidence was high as I drove in to meet the line crew.

Then things began to turn. The first lineman lived near the site and stopped by to view the pole before heading in. He immediately called on his radio, which broadcast to *three* counties. "Who checked this pole? This pole will stand for days like this!"

Turns out, it is almost impossible for a four-way intersection pole to fall. The four attached wires keep the pole steady, even with the bottom severed. The last thing you want to do is change a pole on overtime wages in the middle of the night. My early morning decision to replace the pole became an embarrassing object lesson in overconfidence. A lesson I never again repeated, because the uncomfortable experience stayed with me. Remember the lineman's assurance that the pole would stand for days was broadcast over three counties!

I served as the lead supervisor on call thousands more times, and I always thought back to this moment. This experience may have been a significant ding to my confidence at the time, but the experience gained did much to prepare me for the next issue, and the next. In time, this difficult experience became a source of future confidence.

Because confidence is a feeling, demonstrating confidence is an acquired skill. Sure, one can feel confident with almost no experience. But often we mistake being confident with being cocky. To be cocky is to be confident without a foundation. That missing foundation may be experience, that missing foundation may be knowledge, or that missing foundation may be based upon the advice of others you trust. To be confident without underpinning is to rely on luck for outcomes. While this could be perfectly fine for low-impact choices, this is a recipe for disaster as a leader.

Knowledge serves as an underpinning for confidence. Think about taking tests. Accumulating knowledge through our study and preparation builds understanding and sets the expectation of doing well. Contrast this with those times when we enter tests without adequate preparation. I remember declaring once in college: *Sleep is more important than studying* as I turned in early. Then I tossed and turned all night unable to think of anything but that test! Ever have nightmares where you took a test without being prepared?

Yet there are those times when leaders face circumstances without adequate knowledge or experience. In these situations, leaders must recognize their need to seek help. Contrary to common belief, seeking help as a leader is not a detriment to demonstrating leadership. In these situations, confidence comes from trusting in someone who *does* have experience or knowledge with the given circumstance. This trust may be based on the individual's experience or knowledge, or it may be based solely on the individual's reputation or position. Knowing when and from whom to seek help is a mark of a good leader.

Many good leaders demonstrate confidence in situations, based on their experience, their knowledge, or their ability to trust others. But how does one move from being a good, confident leader to being a good, confident Christian leader? Just like anything else in a Christian life, we rely on God. Consider Proverbs 3:26, the Lord will be our confidence. As a Christian, when we lack experience, when we lack knowledge, and when we cannot find someone to trust, we can always trust in the Lord.

As Christians, we have a source of confidence not available to non-Christians. We have faith, *"the assurance of things hoped for, the evidence of things not seen."*[8] As a Christian, we have a Father who loves us, a Savior who saves us, and a Spirit who guides us. As a Christian, we have a perspective that is broader than this life alone; we have confidence beyond this life. Consider 1 John 5:1-5, which says that *"everyone who has been born of God overcomes the world."* And our faith assures us of that victory.[9] We have victory over this life because of our faith.

---

[8] Hebrews 11:1 *"Now faith is the assurance of things hoped for, the conviction of things not seen."*

[9] 1 John 5:1-5 *"Everyone who believes that Jesus is the Christ has been born of God, and everyone who loves the Father loves whoever has been born of him. By this we know that we love the children of God, when we love God and obey his commandments. For this is the love of God, that we keep his commandments. And his commandments are not burdensome. For everyone who has been born of God overcomes the world. And this is*

These verses in First John teach us to live victoriously in faith. This victory inspired confidence is infectious, a beacon to those who seek refuge and direction. We don't have to declare our confidence aloud, our faces declare confidence, our actions declare confidence. We draw people in with our countenance. This countenance is the difference between a good confident leader, and a good confident Christian leader.

Ask yourself these questions:

- Do I have the experience and knowledge to be confident?
- Do I know when to trust God and others?
- Does my faith translate into a confident countenance before others?

Today, pray for confidence.

Pray that the Holy Spirit will underpin you with a spirit of confidence based on your experience, knowledge, and trust. Pray Proverbs 3:26, that you might count upon the Lord to be your confidence. Confess your shortfalls and pray for improvement. Pray for your leaders to have confidence, pray for your followers to trust your confidence. Pray God will present you with an opportunity to demonstrate confidence. Pray that your countenance reflects your faith and your belief in the victorious life. Finally, thank God for your opportunities and praise Him for His leadership in your life.

---

the victory that has overcome the world—our faith. Who is it that overcomes the world except the one who believes that Jesus is the Son of God?"

DAY FOUR
The First Imperative: Do the Right Thing

BOLDNESS

"Boldness is to dare to bear something difficult."[10]

Biblical Reference: Proverbs 28:1

"The wicked flee when no one pursues, but the righteous are bold as a lion."

Just after 1 A.M., three days before Christmas in 2008, a small flow of coal ash slurry began to seep from a retaining pond outside the TVA Kingston fossil plant. Over the next hour, layer after layer of solid sediment began to liquefy. The small seepage became a torrent. Before sunrise more than 1 billion gallons (1 *billion* gallons!) of coal ash slurry filled the Clinch River basin, washed into surrounding homes, and covered the countryside. This would be the worst coal ash spill in American history. Tom Kilgore was our CEO. The company's legal advisors were clear: Be careful, avoid admission of guilt, and tread lightly. But in one of the boldest decisions in TVA history, Tom Kilgore pulled on his boots, stood amidst the spilled ash, and invited all comers. For the next several days, Kilgore accepted full responsibility without waiting for a person or persons to blame.

There are three essential components of boldness in leadership. First,

---

[10] An Expository Dictionary of New Testament Words, W.E. Vine, 1966.

boldness begins with knowledge. A keen understanding of the risks involved: the potential outcomes and the possible downside. How will this affect the company's reputation? Are we going to be sued? A knowledgeable leader can weigh the risks efficiently and quickly act with boldness without hesitation. The day after the billion gallons of ash slurry, Tom Kilgore boldly stood amidst that spill despite the risks involved.

Secondly, *a bold leader is willing to accept the full consequences,* no matter the outcome. As it turns out, a decision made in the 1970s compromised the strength of the dam, allowing wet slurry to create slippage in the lower levels of the retention pond. The leadership team's decision to slightly alter the original design began a chain of events that led to the spill. This did not matter to Tom Kilgore. "This happened on my watch," he said. "I accept responsibility." He also pledged full and complete restitution for all impacted, including a complete and total restoration of the environment. Almost immediately, the healing began. The recovery cost would crest a billion dollars before completion. Today the site is better than ever, a promise kept by a bold leader, willing to do the opposite of what everyone advised.

Even with deep knowledge and experience, bad things may happen. For bold leaders, like Tom Kilgore, the upside may be outstanding, but the downside could be devastating, potentially bringing financial ruin upon the company. Bold leaders understand and accept the balance of potential upside against what could happen on the downside. It is easy to play it safe, to wait until all the facts are in, to check in with lots of others, to listen to all the advice, as the lawyers and advisors suggested. Safe decisions are often good decisions, but sometimes they miss the mark. Conservative decision-making can lead to lethargic progress, ambiguous direction, and confused followers. Yet sometimes conservative decision-making is the right choice. Bold leaders understand the downside risk and know the timing for either conservative or bold decisions.

The ability to make either conservative or bold decisions is a function of the third component of bold decision making. Trust.

Trust is where the Christian leader has an advantage. God teaches His children to trust. We come to rely on our church, on our fellow Christians, and particularly on our God. That's where Proverbs 28:1 comes in. "The righteous are bold as a lion." As Christians, we have a perspective of the world that is different from non-Christians. As a Christian, we understand

God is at work among us; the Spirit is leading us. When we read the Bible, we understand more about stress and human reactions, foibles, and performance because of this stress.

God fills the Bible with bold leaders who trust God and others to fulfill God's plan for their lives, despite stressful circumstances. Consider Naomi who trusted her relative Boaz to redeem Ruth, a Moabite widow who had few rights in Bethlehem. And consider Esther who trusted her cousin Mordecai's advice to plead with King Ahasuerus for the Jews, even though approaching the king without a summons could mean execution. And finally, Gideon who trusted God to help him overcome the ruling invaders, the Midianites. When we read the Bible, we not only study God, we study mankind. Tom Kilgore, an outstanding Christian leader, understood that only a bold admission of fault would bypass the months of blame and move straight to the healing process. Tom trusted the outcome based on his knowledge, his understanding of the risk, and his trust in mankind to seek the best outcome over the long haul. A Christian leader finds influence through trusting God and others, and this influence augments bold leadership.

Being bold as a leader is tricky. Many confuse boldness with impetuousness. A good leader understands there is more to being bold than simply moving forward with confidence despite the outcome. A bold leader weighs the circumstances and understands the risks. A bold leader analyzes the potential consequences and determines the pathway of greatest success. A bold leader is a leader who trusts the process, or the people associated with the process. Boldness rises from faith, grows through competence, and is demonstrated in the confidence of a well-prepared leader. Being bold doesn't mean ignoring risk. Being bold means rapidly weighing the risks and taking appropriate action alongside the risk. Naomi and Esther took bold action in the face of risk. So did Gideon. So did Tom Kilgore. Build your knowledge, learn to accept the consequences of your actions, and trust in yourself.

Be bold.

Ask yourself these questions:

- Do I have the experience and knowledge to be bold?
- Do I routinely trust God and others with whom I associate?
- Do I play it safe when I know there are opportunities to be bold?

Today, pray that you might be bold at the right time.

Pray that the Holy Spirit might reveal the application of biblical learning to daily situations. Pray Proverbs 28:1, that you might know when to be a lion. Confess your shortfalls and pray for improvement. Pray for your leaders to have boldness, pray for your followers to accept your boldness. Pray God presents you with an opportunity to demonstrate boldness. Finally, thank God for your opportunities and praise Him for His leadership in your life.

DAY FIVE
The First Imperative: Do the Right Thing

ACTION

"Action is the process of getting something done for a particular purpose."[11]

Biblical Reference: James 1:22

"But be doers of the word, and not hearers only, deceiving yourselves."

The title of Superintendent of Engineering, Construction, and Operations, EC&O, was my most descriptive title over forty years of leadership. This moniker meant I looked after about fifty employees in a very small town. This was a hard job, and I was learning on the fly. One of the most difficult actions was ending someone's employment. This kind of serious action requires preparation, and a lot of it. The last thing anyone wants to do is make a hasty decision about something this life altering.

My first experience was excruciating. I hated it. I was slow, checking and rechecking before finally acting. People noticed. Usually by the time someone needs firing, everyone around that person knows it. This is particularly true in the case of line workers. Working on live electricity requires total trust that your fellow worker switched out the right line or

---

[11] https://dictionary.cambridge.org/us/dictionary/english/action

blocked the reclosing function on protecting equipment to prevent the line from reclosing and accidently turning the line back on should a worker contact the energized line. Or maybe a lineman covered the energized line with rubber insulation protection or operated the line truck boom properly while others stood beneath a heavy load. The list of trusted activities is long.

Suffice it to say that line workers often depend on one another for working safely. When line workers can't trust each other, it means more than a bad work environment. It is dangerous. I couldn't afford to be slow when dealing with problems in the line ranks. Over time, experience and knowledge of labor rules improved my speed dealing with problems in the ranks. I also began to learn more about how people behave. Slowly, my speed improved.

Then came a lineman I will call "George." George was a lead line worker on a contract line truck. We contracted with many companies to augment the line worker fleet. George was one such contract worker. I had concerns about George: he made mistakes, some of them safety related. One day George left the office on his way to replace a pole struck by a car the night before. George and his crew had been working all morning and decided to load up and travel down the road for a lunch break. As he drove off, it quickly became apparent that he had forgotten to lower his crane derrick, which allows the line truck to lift loads into place. This crane arm or boom is about twenty-to-thirty feet long. When sticking straight up, as George left it, it is about twenty-five to thirty feet tall! He drove out of the neighborhood without incident, saluting the world with his thirty-foot-tall boom pointing toward the heavens. Unfortunately, as he turned onto the highway, he was not as lucky. As he powered onto the road, his boom caught the power line, the telephone fiber lines, and the cable television lines. The line truck is a formidable vehicle. George successfully severed all those lines and pulled over the adjacent pole. Not only was the neighborhood in the dark, without power and communications, but George had interrupted half the county!

I happened to be in my company vehicle at the time, making my own way to lunch. When the radio erupted, I knew something was wrong. It wasn't far to where George was working, so I made my way to the site. At this point, all my preparation and knowledge on labor laws and employee behavior fed the need for immediate action. I fired George as we stood in the middle of the now blocked highway. This action was essential for his safety as well as the safety of those around him. Later that day, post-George, I got a call from the "big boss". Turns out I made a mistake. I couldn't fire a contractor, only the contractor's management company could fire him.

Whoops.

I called the contractor's big boss and apologized. This gave me the opportunity to make sure he understood my position on George's lack of focus as a line worker. I took action. Someone had too. All fifty people working for me understood the need for action and applauded the results. My superintendent peers got a good chuckle out of my mistake. Of course, I made the "big boss" nervous, not to mention the contract company's management team. But despite a lot of raised eyebrows, we took action immediately that would normally take days. After this incident, new rules gave superintendents the authority to remove contractors from the premises. This new rule thrilled my chuckling peers. I had always thought of that particular rule as a technicality, just do the right thing.

Doing the right thing starts with *doing*. Many leaders find themselves caught up by inaction, unable to make something happen. People follow people when they make things happen. But making things happen can be extraordinarily challenging, particularly in this data-rich, analytical world. There is always more data, more information available. At times we focus more on accumulating data than understanding what the data tells us. Those of us in the engineering profession are considerably guilty in this respect. We seem to think precision comes from the acquisition of more and more research, often well beyond the requirements for the task at hand. I once argued with an employee who was continuing to fine tune an overdue cost estimate, even after I had explained plus or minus ten percent was perfectly fine for the situation. Leaders find themselves caught between enough and maybe needing more. The best leaders capably maneuver through this complexity to make risk-informed choices with the best information available—and make their decisions quickly.

Certainly, some people are naturally action-oriented, but for most of us taking action is an acquired skill. In either case, taking action comes with a host of dangers, particularly as decisions grow in complexity. It is therefore important to develop the skills necessary to filter information rapidly, to simplify complexity, and to move at speeds commensurate to the risk. While this may seem a difficult concept, speed is a skill that requires advanced preparation.

When we have less knowledge on issues, more preparation becomes very important. For example, my knowledge level is low on mortgages. I can help offset that lack of knowledge by studying about mortgages. Even though I study and prepare, I am unlikely to become as knowledgeable as someone who lives with mortgages daily, say a mortgage officer. This is where anticipation prepares us for action. By looking forward and thinking through possible situations I may face when seeking a mortgage, I can be better prepared to act quickly when a mortgage officer asks, "Do you want a fixed or variable rate?"

In other words, when faced with complex decisions, prepare in advance to compensate where your knowledge is lacking. This approach pays dividends in faster decision making for leaders. Of course, there are times for unanticipated, spontaneous decisions. Decisions like firing George on the spot. In these circumstances little preparation time is available, so honing our skills of anticipation and preparation mold an action process that begins to shape leader response. Over time even spontaneous decisions flow freely from rapid evaluation.

Again, action is an area where Christians have an advantage. Consider our focus verse, James 1:22. Mature Christians become doers of the Word, not only hearers of the Word. We have practice. And practice leads to speed. The Bible teaches us to have an actionable faith, a faith that produces. James goes on in chapter two, verse fourteen, to challenge the validity of faith when there are no works. *"What good is it, my brothers, if someone says he has faith but does not have works? Can that faith save him?"* James teaches us that faith leads to action.

All through the Bible, God uses people of action. People like Stephen who died a martyr because of his actions to tell the Jewish people about Christ. People like Isaiah who spoke the truth about animal sacrifices and idol worship to an unhearing, rebellious audience. How about David, the shepherd boy who took on the giant Goliath. Or Peter, whose confident speaking and bold actions before the Pharisees established him as the leader of the early church. God loves people who act, who make a difference by their actions. As we read the Word, the Word intermingles with our spirit. God's Word shapes us and provides perspective that reaches beyond the norm. As we hide the Word in our hearts, the Holy Spirit recalls these words to feed our clarity.

And clarity stimulates action!

Ask yourself these questions:

- Do I over-analyze situations?
- Do I spend enough time in God's Word to internalize those teachings?
- Do I practice preparation and knowledge to improve speed in decision-making?

Today, pray for the ability to take effective action.

Pray that the Holy Spirit will make the complex simple and give you clarity. Pray that you learn to anticipate and prepare. Pray James 1:22, that you become a doer of the Word, not only a listener. Confess your shortfalls and pray for improvement. Pray for your leaders to take effective action, pray for your followers to trust your actions. Pray God will present you with an opportunity to take an informed action. Pray that you understand the balance between too slow and too fast. Finally, thank God for your opportunities and praise Him for His leadership in your life.

DAY SIX
The First Imperative: Do the Right Thing

TOUGH AND GENTLE

To be tough is to "be physically and emotionally strong."[12] *To be gentle is to "be free from harshness, sternness or violence."*[13]

Biblical Reference: 2 Timothy 2:15

"Do your best to present yourself to God as one approved, a worker who has no need to be ashamed, rightly handling the word of truth."

Managing people is tough. Over almost forty years, I found a routine, a comfort level in even the most difficult circumstances. Over the years, I counseled employees for drug use, for alcoholism, for lewd behavior, for pornography. I have reconciled physical fights, psychological fights, email fights, telephone fights, you name it. It is never easy to embrace conflict and take it on. Yet, if you are effective, you look conflict in the eyes and tough your way through. Although sometimes, you can't tough your way through, you have to gentle your way through.

Ending someone's employment is always a difficult challenge. Most

---

[12] https://www.merriam-webster.com/dictionary/tough
[13] https://www.merriam-webster.com/dictionary/gentle

of the time, it requires a great deal of thought and preparation, although sometimes, like in the case of George, you just have to act. One of my preparations before terminating someone was always trying to anticipate their reaction and preparing for that reaction. More than once, this enabled me to hold my cool, or my professionalism.

I knew one fellow was going to get mad, and when he stood and pounded on my desk, I was mentally prepared, and already had a response ready. Angry ones I could handle with ease. The harder ones just sat quietly, or worse, shed tears. Those knowing their deserved fate often cried, disappointed more with themselves than my actions against them. As my experience with this awful activity grew, I found just being a fellow human being was the best approach. There were people who needed a tough taskmaster. They just wanted me to state the reasons clearly and go through the next steps one at a time. Then others needed emotional support, looking for someone to help them see it was going to be okay. They needed someone gentle. The key was knowing when to be tough and when to be gentle.

It's funny, I don't remember much about those times when I had to be tough. I find it easier to be tough. There is less emotional baggage in being tough. Being tough is about preparation and anticipation and sticking to the script. After forty years, I can be tough with my eyes closed. Being tough is easy. What's really hard is being gentle. I will never forget the gentle experiences.

My most vivid memory of this kind of event goes back many years. I knew the action I was taking would devastate the life of "Jennifer". She entered the room crying. We both knew she was guilty; we both knew there was no other option. But we also both knew the implications that would follow. I delivered the message as gentle as I could. Then I asked her how she felt. She kept crying. Not a loud cry, but the quiet, rolling sob that rips your heart out. What she told me will stay with me forever. "All my hope was in that job. All my hope for me, all my hope for my son. Now it's gone."

I couldn't help it. I cried with her. The HR[14] rep was terrified. I asked her to please find help, I promised to pray for her, and I held her hand as we walked to the door. I haven't seen her since.

---

[14] HR is "Human Resources", we all have HR, right?

For many like me, it is easy to be tough. For others, it is easy to be gentle. There are many tough leaders and many gentle leaders. The ability to be *both* tough and gentle differentiates the ordinary leader from the special leader.

The world largely honors tough leaders, those who take no prisoners, raising companies from mediocre performance to deliver exceptional results. The tough leader does not back down from any challenge. The tough leader takes on all opponents with zeal and passion. But the tough leader abuses people. The tough leader treats people as interchangeable parts. The tough leader wears out the parts, throws them away, and replaces them with new parts. The financial world loves these kinds of leaders. Corporations love these kinds of leaders. Employees hate them.

Unfortunately, the purely gentle leader isn't much better. The gentle leader runs from conflict and tolerates poor behavior and performance. The gentle leader can be inconsistent with results, vacillating on decisions or choices depending on the difficulty of the circumstances. The gentle leader treats everyone with respect and appreciation. Gentle leaders endear themselves to employees who love gentle leaders. Employees are often friends with gentle leaders, *but* they seldom follow them well.

The marriage of tough and gentle requires a combination of skill and timing. Toughness can be an acquired skill for the naturally gentle, just as gentleness can be an acquired skill for the tough. There are methods for learning both skills, just as there are times for using one but not the other skill. For the gentle nature, a prepared list of actions, even a prepared script, can teach toughness. Likewise, for the tough at heart, a constant reminder to be sure and consider the human factor can teach gentleness. These are actions we practice, learn, and internalize. As we improve at utilizing both, we find our timing.

Balancing tough and gentle always brings to mind the apostle Paul who encouraged Timothy to rightly handle the Word of truth. Sometimes Paul was tough, very tough, as with John Mark. Paul insisted that John Mark stay behind as Paul and Barnabas left for Antioch, because John Mark had abandoned their work before, for reasons Luke chose not to document. Paul believed John Mark should not join them. The argument was so intense Paul and Barnabas went separate ways. Paul could be very tough. But sometimes Paul was gentle, easy, with his followers, as in 1

Thessalonians 2:7, *"We were gentle among you, like a nursing mother taking care of her own children."*

Gentle Jesus directs us to turn the other cheek,[15] but tough Jesus overthrows the tables of the money lenders in the temple and stands before the Sanhedrin defiantly in silence until He decides the time to speak the truth, knowing exactly what the truth brings. Christian leaders must rightly handle the truth. I admit that sometimes the truth demands a tough response, sometimes a gentle response. Learn to deliver either toughness or gentleness or both together, praying for the Holy Spirit to direct you.

Ask yourself these questions:

- Do I have the skills to be both tough and gentle?
- Do I consistently discern the right approach at the right time?
- Do I listen as the Holy Spirit guides me?

Today, pray for the ability to be both tough and gentle.

Pray that the Holy Spirit will guide you in appropriate timing. Pray 2 Timothy 2:15, that you might rightly handle the truth. Confess your shortfalls and pray for improvement. Pray for those who lead you to possess the skill to be both tough and gentle, pray for your followers to accept your discernment. Pray God will present you with an opportunity to demonstrate both tough and gentle skills. Finally, thank God for your opportunities and praise Him for His leadership in your life.

---

[15] Matthew 5:39 (ESV) "But *I say to you, do not resist the one who is evil. But if anyone slaps you on the right cheek, turn to him the other also.*"

DAY SEVEN
The First Imperative: Do the Right Thing

PERSEVERANCE

"Perseverance is the continued effort to achieve something despite difficulties, failure or opposition."[16]

Biblical Reference: Hebrews 12:1-2

"Therefore, since we are surrounded by so great a cloud of witnesses, let us also lay aside every weight, and sin which clings so closely, and let us run with endurance the race that is set before us, looking to Jesus, the founder and perfecter of our faith, who for the joy that was set before him endured the cross, despising the shame, and is seated at the right hand of the throne of God."

Electromagnetic Fields were not my friends when I was in college. At twenty-one years old, I was in over my head in Bud Flood's Electromagnetic Fields I class at North Carolina State. I tried hard. I studied. I sought guidance. But the topic just didn't click. The mid-term exam was exasperating. Well, at least the results were exasperating. I scored thirty-eight. Out of 100!

Unfortunately, this low grade was a reasonable reflection of my

---

[16] https://www.merriam-webster.com/dictionary/perseverance

understanding of electromagnetic fields. However, on my review of the test I found that I had made a minor mathematical mistake on one of the four problems. Often professors are willing to offer partial credit if you demonstrate an understanding of the issue and simply make a minor error of mathematics. My process was sound, but the execution was slightly askew. I immediately scheduled a conference with Professor Flood. I waited almost an hour outside his office, building up my confidence and laying out my plea. When the time came, he listened intently, even asked me follow-up questions.

At the end he asked me one specific question. "Is the answer correct?" Of course, there was only one answer to that question, not the one written on my test. He smiled and said in a rich, New Jersey baritone, "You know, son, I respect you for coming in here, and that was a really good speech. I can see you understood this question, so I am going to give you a break." He took my exam and with a big red, permanent marker crossed out the thirty-eight and replaced it with a forty-two!

That semester I made a *D* in Electromagnetic Fields. I would like to say that was my only *D* at NC State, but I made another the next semester. Electromagnetic Fields II.

Later I signed on to work at Duke Power and forgot all I knew about electromagnetic fields. Within a few years, however, people began to ask questions about the fields near utility lines. By this time, I had a good bit of experience as a spokesperson on technical issues, and I ended up representing Duke in several forums to speak as an "expert" on electromagnetic fields. I spoke, but I still didn't really understand the science behind my words.

At TVA, I had much the same experience, only with higher voltages, and subsequently higher electromagnetic fields. Then something unexpected happened. I retired from TVA and joined the Electric Power Research Institute (EPRI). One of the hot issues of the day was the impact of nuclear weapons on the earth's electromagnetic fields. I was soon spearheading a multi-million-dollar electromagnetic pulse (EMP) project. This time, I sat with some very bright folks who walked me through the topic bit by bit. After forty years, electromagnetic fields finally clicked. I couldn't believe I understood electromagnetic fields. I would later testify before the Senate

Energy Committee representing the Electric Utility industry as an expert on Electromagnetic Fields and EMP.

Bud Flood would be proud!

Perseverance is not unyielding stubbornness. I was *never* going to get electromagnetic fields in the 1970s. It took a lifetime of experience. You can't plan your way to perseverance. Perseverance is knowing when to let go and when to hold on. But once you hold on, know how to hold on without alienating people around you. Avoid running over people with your perseverance. Keep your emotions in check as you argue your point. Concede the good points of others. And never advance a topic obviously out-of-sync with the organization you serve. Instead watch for the right time. Once in a while, you may have to create that time with a breakthrough. I created breakthroughs like this by involving other key leaders, seeking advocates and building momentum. Most often, like my efforts to understand EMP, the right time comes to you. What is important is to stay with it as long as it feels like the right thing to do. I quietly persevered in my knowledge of electromagnetic fields for forty years. And that perseverance paid off in my service to the Electric Power Research Institute and my country as we fortified the grid against EMP weapons.

Business success requires perseverance, leader or not. Often though, the leader must endure and persevere beyond the follower. When followers tire of repeated failure, the leader steps up or steps down. Sometimes it is time to step down, like accepting *D's* in electromagnetic fields classes when you just don't get it. If something just won't work, then continuing to bang one's head against the wall only brings a giant headache. Nonetheless, many great successes occur only after everyone else has given up and one last person perseveres, like my friends at EPRI who finally found a way to teach me electromagnetic fields. A great part of the leader's role is to understand the trade-off between continuing to press hard forward, and when to stop altogether. This is a difficult skill and comes with practice and knowledge, coupled with a sense of doing the right thing.

The apostle Paul writes in our focus verse that we are to run the race (of life) with endurance. When we think of endurance racing, we think of the marathon, or the longer challenges, and not the sprints. Many times, life presents us with challenges that may look like sprints but are instead brutal marathons. In these times perseverance is invaluable.

Jimmy Valvano expressed perseverance in a wonderful way as he was dying from cancer when he encouraged others to never give up.[17] Coach Valvano used the 1983 National Championship team from NC State as an example of perseverance. In particular, the double overtime victory over Pepperdine in the West Regional. I watched that game on television late at night in Hickory, North Carolina. I must admit. I almost gave up. I had to work the next morning and it was 1 A.M. I started to go to bed but changed my mind and hung with them. NC State miraculously pulled out a victory because they never gave up! They persevered.

Christian leaders possess an eternal perspective that provides fuel for perseverance. Just look at the book of Hebrews, written to a group of new Christians who were challenged to live their faith amidst daily persecution. They operated largely by word of mouth and letters. Yet the Holy Spirit and the encouragement of fellow believers kept them pressing forward to establish a Christian stronghold among the Hebrew people.

The Christian leader expects life to be challenging, to be a marathon, not a sprint. We understand even as we run the race, the Lord seeks to perfect us to become all He created us to be. We run with joy because we understand what lies at the finish. This joy, when coupled with an eternal perspective, offers Christian leaders the opportunity to hang in there when others bail out. Take advantage of this experience and leverage perseverance in your work life, just as you leverage perseverance in your spiritual life.

Ask yourself these questions:

- Do I know when to hang on and when to let go?
- Do I understand God's timing and look to advance issues only when the time is right?
- Do I persevere with joy and humbleness or with whining and complaints?

---

[17] "Don't Give Up...Don't Ever Give Up", by Justin and Robyn Spizman, 2009.

Today, pray for perseverance.

Pray that the Holy Spirit will give you the wisdom to discern when you should stop and when you should continue on. Pray Hebrews 12:1-2: that you might endure with great joy. Confess your shortfalls and pray for improvement. Pray for your leaders to have staying power in difficult circumstances, pray for your followers to accept the race you run. Pray God will present you with an opportunity to demonstrate perseverance. Pray that your joy might reflect Christ in your life so that you might be a witness even as you persevere. Finally, thank God for your opportunities and praise Him for His leadership in your life.

DAY EIGHT
The First Imperative: Do the Right Thing

PRESENCE

"Presence is the bearing, carriage or air of a person."[18]

Biblical Reference: Exodus 33:14

"And he said, 'My presence will go with you, and I will give you rest.'"

There was a time when every vice president at Duke Power Company was tall. Not just a little tall, 6'3" or greater kind of tall. They had presence. They were big. When they walked into a room, heads turned. When they spoke, people listened. Lucky for Duke, these tall people were also pretty good leaders. Lucky for me, Duke learned there is more to having presence than physical bearing.

Near the end of my career, while I was at the Electric Power Research Institute (EPRI), I had the honor of testifying before Senate committees as a utility expert. I did so on three occasions. The last Senate Committee hearing was on the impact of EMP to the electric grid. This issue was heating up at the time as North Korea continued to test nuclear weapons capable of delivering EMP impact to the United States. At the hearing, the room was full of media and political staff. On the panel with me

---

[18] https://www.merriam-webster.com/dictionary/presence

was a commissioner from the Federal Energy Regulatory Commission, a retired admiral—now EMP Protection advocate, the CEO of an electric utility, and Newt Gingrich, former Speaker of the House. This was an intimidating group.

Had I been part of this panel early in my career I would have been terrified, but after thirty-five years, I knew better. I had become an EMP spokesperson for EPRI. Coupled with my utility background, I knew more about how EMP specifically impacted the grid than anyone in the room. I practiced my three-minute opening until I could do it with no notes, and I prepared almost 100 sample questions and answers beforehand. This level of preparation had me looking forward to the senators' questions. I entered the room with presence. Not because of who I was, but because I was ready and confident. All my nerves and apprehension gave way to anticipation. This experience was one of the highlights of my forty years in the business.

We all know people with a natural presence. When they walk into a room, the mood changes, conversations wane. Some of these folks make good leaders, but not all. Even though presence is natural for many, presence is also a learned skill. You don't have to be 6'3" tall or have a naturally magnetic personality. You can work on your presence, no matter where you begin.

Presence starts with how you interact with people. The presence you project for a meeting with a peer team may be different from a meeting with employees to deal with performance issues. Presence also starts by thinking about your purpose. Think about your objective and ask yourself, "What would I as an employee look for in my leader were I in his or her place?"

There are many variations, but a few foundational approaches help in most circumstances. This begins with your own comfort. You must in all cases appear relaxed. Even if you are nervous, find a way to appear more relaxed. If you are giving a speech, practice until you know what you want to say inside out. If you are answering questions, devise sample questions and prepare your responses in advance. If you are holding a round-table discussion with employees, know what you want to say, know what their big issues are, and prepare by centering yourself around your message. Extensive preparation will help you relax. People will notice you are relaxed, and form perspectives based on their observations.

You must also be engaging. This is an active word. Move around if possible, actively make eye contact. Listen actively, shaking your head yes or no and asking for clarification on issues you wonder about. If you are good with humor, you can inject humor. If you are not, avoid it. Leave your notes on the stand and make it seem as if you are so confident, so knowledgeable, that you don't need notes to keep you on track. Vary your voice so people stay engaged. If you find yourself losing the group, take a long pause, or raise your voice for a moment, or speak very quietly until eyes begin to follow you. Your objective is to own the room, and this takes work.

If you aren't leading the meeting, sit on the right of the leader, about midway. If the leader is left-handed, sit on the left. This is where the leader's eyes first look, and, therefore, the eyes of those attending the meeting also naturally fall here. As you listen in the meeting, know what points you want to make and how you will make them. Insert them at an appropriate time, again with good eye contact and active listening.

Finally, you must be open and in control. Just because others may become agitated doesn't mean you need to follow suit. Stay in control no matter what happens in the meeting. A calm measured approach is almost always better. Even on the rare occasion when you may need to ramp up your passion for motivational reasons, do so under full control. Let people talk, acknowledge their contributions, and always consider improving your position by incorporating the input of others.

In Exodus 33:14, God promises Moses, *"My presence will go with you, and I will give you rest."* You may know the story well. God appeared to him and the Israelites he was leading as a pillar of clouds in the day and a pillar of fire by night. What an encouragement this must have been for Moses to clearly see he was walking with the Lord. He was clearly in God's presence. This was Moses's rest. God took pressure off Moses and took the pressure Himself.

The presence of the Lord is also with you. Scripture maintains that it is *"no longer you who live but Christ who lives within you."*[19] Peter speaks of the times of refreshing that come from the Lord.[20] Claim God's presence.

---

[19] Galatians 2:20

[20] Acts 3:20 *"that times of refreshing may come from the presence of the Lord, and that he may send the Christ appointed for you, Jesus."*

Call on the Lord to give you refreshment, energy, recall, and confidence. Your presence comes from these qualities. God's presence comes from His amazing omnipotent power and love.

Your presence comes from hard work!

Ask yourself these questions:

- How do those who follow me see me?
- Do I have weaknesses that deter from the presence I desire to reflect?
- Have I asked God to keep me in His presence and give me rest?

Today, pray for presence.

Pray that the Holy Spirit will help with the skills needed to convey the presence you desire. Pray Exodus 33:14, that you might call on the Lord to keep you in His presence and give you rest. Confess your shortfalls and pray for improvement. Pray for the presence of your leaders, pray for your followers to see your heart. Pray God will present you with an opportunity to demonstrate presence. Pray that practicing presence makes the skill more intuitive in your role as a leader. Finally, thank God for your opportunities and praise Him for His leadership in your life.

DAY NINE
The First Imperative: Do the Right Thing

BELIEVE

> *"To believe is to hold something as the truth."*[21]

Biblical Reference: 1 Thessalonians 2:13

> *"And we also thank God constantly for this, that when you received the word of God, which you heard from us, you accepted it not as the word of men but as what it really is, the word of God, which is at work in you believers."*

For most of us, belief is the easy part, but living like we believe is far more challenging. This is particularly true for leaders, because other people often carefully notice their actions. At TVA, I developed a habit of leaving work about 5:15 P.M., finding dinner at a nearby restaurant before the crowds, and then returning to the office to wrap up the day.

One day a young lady highlighted my behavior in a letter to the CEO. "He leaves every day at 5:15. How does someone in his position get to just leave like that when I am constantly working late to get my job done?" This young lady didn't know I arrived an hour before everyone else, and she was gone when I returned after dinner. In her eyes, I was lazy, cutting out early

---

[21] https://www.merriam-webster.com/dictionary/believe

every day. Her perspective reflected the example I set through the schedule I followed. I put in my time and more, but this young lady never saw the extra time. I changed my behavior to make what I did more apparent. I began staying longer, only about a half hour. During that half hour most everyone left. Dinner was a little later and my routine was disrupted, but the example greatly improved.

The lesson for me: People watch their leaders.

So how do you as a Christian demonstrate your Christian walk as people are watching your every move? Lucky for us, God gives us a manual. Just like your company has a safety manual or a Human Resources Manual, God gives you a manual for behavior, which we call the Holy Bible. God's word is our gift to help in our lives. As First Thessalonians 2:13 tells us, God's word is at work in believers. *But* this is only evident when God's believers are at work in God's word.

If you want to strengthen your belief, open the Bible regularly. Study the manual. Learn the rules, guides, and helps that thousands of years of God-inspired history provide you. It's the first step to living like a Christian. Only then can you begin to consider leading like a Christian.

To be effective Christian leaders, we must first be effective Christians who know what we believe. Our foundational theology is different from all other religions and beliefs. Christians believe and worship God the Father, Christ the Son, and the Holy Spirit. Christians acknowledge the failure of men and women to adhere to God's law, resulting in a need for redemption before a Holy God. Christians recognize Jesus as the Messiah, the Christ, sent to earth to live as fully man, yet fully God. Christians know Jesus gave His life in perfect sacrifice on the cross as redemption for the sin of all believers. That same Jesus defeated death three days later so all who believe may also defeat death. That same Jesus will come again to call all who believe to His side in ultimate victory against evil.

If you are uncomfortable or unfamiliar with this, the gospel message, then it will be difficult to serve as a Christian leader. This doesn't mean you cannot lead. On the contrary, there are many effective, good, even great leaders who are not Christians. But if you struggle with the conflict between worldly leadership and Christianity, God has a plan for you. God has a plan to help you as a leader be a light to the world by demonstrating your Christianity in how you lead.

If you don't know if you are a Christian or not, then I invite you to walk the Roman Road. In Paul's letter to the Roman church, he lays out a clear pathway to faith in Jesus. Begin in Romans 3:23, "*for all have sinned and fall short of the glory of God.*" You are not alone in your sin. Move ahead to Romans 5:8, "*but God shows his love for us in that while we were still sinners, Christ died for us.*" God understands our condition and has a solution. Romans 6:23 outlines the remedy for our condition: "*For the wages of sin is death, but the free gift of God is eternal life in Christ Jesus our Lord.*" This path to eternal life is free. Romans 10:9 confirms this free gift: "*because, if you confess with your mouth that Jesus is Lord and believe in your heart that God raised him from the dead, you will be saved.*" Romans 10:13 provides the final assurance of your salvation: "*For everyone who calls on the name of the Lord will be saved.*"

God is always ready to accept you as a member of His family. Pray and confess your sins, your need for Christ. You can do this right now. Ask for salvation and it is given. Find a local church that teaches the Bible and talk with a pastor. Giving your life to Christ is the beginning of a new life, a life filled with the Holy Spirit. A life ready to be used as a leader doing God's work.

The gospel message is a simple message. God does the work, you simply believe. Then you live like you believe.

Ask yourself these questions:

- Am I comfortable in what I believe about Christianity?
- Do I spend enough time in God's Word that these words guide my heart and my decisions?
- Are there opportunities to improve my knowledge and understanding of the Bible and its application to my circumstances?

Today, pray for your belief.

Pray that the Holy Spirit will increase your faith and strengthen your belief. Pray First Thessalonians 2:13, that you might embrace the word of God as a work in your life. Confess your shortfalls and pray for improvement. Pray for your leaders to believe, pray for your followers to believe. Pray God will present you with an opportunity to demonstrate your belief. Pray that your belief is stronger than the challenges that come upon you. Finally, thank God for the opportunities you have and praise Him for His leadership in your life.

DAY TEN
Imperative Two: Know the Right thing To Do

Biblical Reference: Job 12:13

"With God are wisdom and might; He has counsel and understanding."

Called "The Super Outbreak," the storm on April 27, 2011, remains the worst tornado outbreak in United States history, devastating the U.S. Southeast. I stood in the TVA Control Center with the Operations team. Across the front of the huge room stood the giant electronic board. This board was a real time map of the TVA system, complete with green lights for energized lines and red for de-energized lines. We stood watching as transmission line after line went red. Within a few hours, all of Mississippi was red. Soon all of Alabama. Most of Georgia. And a good bit of Tennessee. By the third day, we had a good handle on the recovery, except for one very difficult place. Huntsville, Alabama. Every single feed into the city of Huntsville was not only down but destroyed.

After a very difficult call with the Huntsville office late at night, Bob, my VP of Operations, and I sat at the whiteboard and began to sketch out the options. The office was dark, except for our conference room as we worked scenario after scenario. No matter what we did, we could not find a way to bring Huntsville online and meet the minimum requirements of grid interconnection. About 3 A.M., our energy was gone, and we left for the night with no solution.

The next morning Bob came running into my office. He had thought of a solution while showering that morning. If we could get the 500,000-volt line up from Widows Creek, Alabama, to Huntsville, we could set the protection scheme to lock out the circuit if anything happened. That just means we put the equivalent of a really big fuse in the line feeding Huntsville. In the business we call that "one shot to lockout." This solution protected the rest of the grid and got Huntsville back days earlier than we thought possible. Huntsville residents hung out there at the mercy of a single 80-mile line set to de-energize on the slightest event. But they had power. The line stayed up until we could rebuild other feeds and no one in Huntsville ever knew how precarious their situation was. This approach was the right thing to do, which came from late-night scenario building and one early morning epiphany.

Our First Imperative—"Doing the Right Thing"—can be hard work. Doing the right thing starts with your belief and integrity. Your confidence and boldness molds you to do the right thing, and your speed and action provide demonstrations of your commitment. In doing the right thing you focus mostly on how you interact with people and rules. You execute toughness with a gentle touch. Doing the right thing underscores your presence and rewards your perseverance. Doing the right thing is difficult.

But for Christian leaders, our Second Imperative— "Knowing What to Do"—is even more difficult. It is impossible to do the right thing unless you *know what the right thing is,* which may not be readily apparent. You see shades of right battling with shades of wrong so strongly that no clear winner emerges. This is particularly true for Christians who must factor in moral and spiritual obligation along the way.

Sorting through complexity requires careful introspection. Like Bob, who went to sleep unable to identify the right answer. But with a night of rest, and a long history of experience and knowledge, he figured out exactly what we needed. We went to bed thinking it would be three days before restoring power to Huntsville, and within hours the next morning, we had a plan for full restoration by the end of the day.

Think of knowing the right thing to do as primarily back-office work. This is the work done at night when all is quiet, like Bob and I that night in 2011, or work done in small groups, driving to greater levels of understanding. This kind of work often goes unnoticed. People don't see the preparation time or the research and reading. What others see is the execution of the right thing, easily, seamlessly, apparently with little effort—while under the surface you are scrambling to put the pieces together.

Our TVA engineers and linemen met Bob's idea with roaring support. The City of Huntsville was ecstatic. Bob emerged a respected leader, a man people yearned to follow. Somehow leaders like Bob always have a pathway forward, no matter how difficult the task. People line up behind these kinds of leaders.

As a Christian leader, you have the benefit of asking for help that you can consistently rely upon. After all, God is the source of wisdom and understanding. Yet relying on God does not replace building your own wisdom and understanding with the information and tools at hand. Prayer and the guidance of the Holy Spirit are certainly helpful in dealing with hard choices. But the Holy Spirit has much more substance for you when you take the time to seriously analyze situations and circumstances.

Knowing the right thing to do requires specific skills and attributes. The following attributes provide a strong foundation for discerning the right thing. These attributes are intelligence, patience, listening skills, self-awareness, problem-solving skills, discernment, and calmness so you can make intelligent decisions, no matter the crisis. We will explore each of these attributes over the next several days. Knowing the right thing to do is hard, but essential. Without wisdom and understanding, wrong things happen. It doesn't take many wrong decisions to lose your followers.

Today, pause and pray that you understand how to discern the right thing to do.

Pray that the words on these pages serve as guides to reveal the Spirit's direction for your actions. Pray that opportunities present themselves that you might demonstrate and remember the things you learn. Pray for your leaders, pray for your followers, pray for yourself, that you might fully align with God's plan. Finally, thank God for your opportunities and praise Him for His leadership in your life.

DAY ELEVEN
Imperative Two: Know the Right Thing To Do

INTELLIGENCE

> *"Intelligence is the ability to acquire and apply knowledge and skills."*[22]

Biblical Reference: James 3:13 NIV

> *"Who is wise and understanding among you? Let them show it by their good life, by deeds done in the humility that comes from wisdom."*

Bill Johnson was my first *new* CEO at TVA. I was comfortable with my old CEO. I respected my old CEO. When he retired, all of TVA was concerned about who might follow. Bill was not what we expected. Bill played football at Penn State, a big man with a personality to match his physical presence. Within a few days we found him to be a natural leader, easy to follow, an imposing figure who drew people with ease. Yet underneath the easygoing, likable guy was an extraordinary intelligence and a quick wit. Bill had the ability to pick up information quickly and just as quickly assimilate and deal with it. He moved fast. TVA was not fast. Yet under Bill's leadership, TVA became fast, or at least faster. Bill was one of the industry's first CEO's to recognize and act to shift away from coal

---

[22] https://en.oxforddictionaries.com/definition/intelligence

for power generation. His press for speed placed TVA years ahead of other utilities. He left the TVA in 2018 after six extraordinary years.

One of Bill's quiet skills was a method he used to evaluate talent. When he met new people, Bill would offer an unusual joke, often with an obscure punch line. Or maybe just an unexpected quip. He would watch to see if people "got it." Once I caught on, I watched Bill do this over and over again. He was judging intelligence. By sharing these complex stories, he could quickly tell whose mind moved at sufficient speed to track with him. Bill knew TVA needed to reduce the size of its management team, and he wanted intelligence speed in those who stuck long term. As we began to downsize the workforce, I observed the effectiveness of his approach. He was right more than not with his measure of intelligence speed.

Psychology Today recently argued that the best leader for a group has only slightly greater intelligence than the average intelligence of the group.[23] Leaders with considerably higher intelligence tend to over-complicate circumstances or communication, leaving followers confused and annoyed. Those with considerably lower intelligence tend to appear inadequate or underprepared when followers challenge them. In truth, intelligence is far more than the historically measured intelligence quotient or IQ. Leadership intelligence is about wisdom, understanding what is happening around you, and how you apply that wisdom and understanding. In particular, how fast you can apply those characteristics to the circumstances around you. In other words, speed.

Intelligence comes from many sources. Bill is very intelligent naturally, earning a law degree, but he also gained intelligence from his experience at the helm of multiple companies. Intelligence is not really a measure of how smart you are. Intelligence requires a willingness and ability to gain wisdom and understanding. Those who lack the willingness to learn quickly lose the ability to engage effectively with others, falling behind peers and followers. Learning comes easier to some than others. Perhaps you learn quickly, or perhaps you work very hard to learn. In the end it matters little how you acquire the knowledge needed, only that you are willing and able to do so.

Which brings me back to Bill Johnson. Bill valued speed of intelligence,

---

[23] Psychology Today: "How Smart Should a Leader Be?", Romeo Vitelli, PhD, August 7, 2017

not simply intelligence alone. Leaders must pace workers, or if possible, stay slightly ahead. In other words, you need to be able to think fast to effectively lead. One must rapidly assimilate circumstances and deal effectively with them. Speed of understanding requires practice, good listening skills, and a general knowledge of the issue or issues. Speed may come naturally, or it may be extraordinarily difficult. Either way, speed is a critical part of effective leadership.

But what about the wisdom mentioned in James 3:13? Wisdom sounds like a biblical word, but you don't have to be a biblical scholar to gain wisdom. Many secular leaders have accumulated great wisdom. Yet, as a Christian leader, you have a perspective that secular leaders lack. You have Psalm 94:11: *"The LORD knows the thoughts of man, that they are a mere breath."* In other words, you know how to keep your own wisdom in perspective. After all, the Bible clearly tells us God considers our greatest wisdom but a mere breath. Christian leaders are comfortable recognizing there are others smarter. As Christians we recognize our own wisdom is never as great as it can be. This perspective leads us to embrace learning. This is a great assistance in coupling wisdom with understanding and application. The grasp of all three are necessary for speed.

Assuming you have the willingness to learn and acquire wisdom, and you develop a reasonable speed of understanding, you only need to apply that wisdom and understanding properly. This is where you have a distinct advantage as a Christian leader. James tells us in 3:13 to show wisdom by your good life. James calls out deeds done in the humility that comes from wisdom. Not the deeds done so all can see and bring accolades upon the doer. Instead James points to quiet deeds, behind the scenes work that often goes unnoticed. James describes the kind of deeds that cause people to look at you and know you are a good person. Not because of some wonderful thing that you have done, but because of a series of actions that individually go unnoticed, yet together they add up to a positive countenance, a clear label as a good person. As a leader, this might manifest as a boss's or employee's positive reinforcement, an encouragement, a pat on the back.

My first CEO at TVA, Tom Kilgore used to call or visit the Control Room staff on Christmas day each year. These people wanted to be with their families on Christmas, but instead were working. Tom knew that, and quietly gave up part of his own family Christmas to stop by or call, telling these employees how much he appreciated their work on Christmas day. Good people and good leaders have a lot in common. Each recognizes the need for small deeds like James describes. And as James says, these small deeds demonstrate your good life, while emanating from the humility that is only gained from wisdom. The ability to absorb wisdom, to ingest understanding and allow wisdom to shape how you interact with people and situations, is a clear sign of Christian maturity. It is one thing to learn, understand, and develop action plans. It is quite another to take knowledge and understanding, overlay it on the circumstances and people all about you, and rapidly apply what you know.

The mature Christian leader molds the application of knowledge and understanding to fit the team. The Bible calls it good behavior. This is a way of getting things done with gentleness and appreciation rather than manipulation and aggression. Good behavior is a sign of someone seeking to emulate Christ. To live is Christ, Paul reminds us.

Society seeks to convince us intelligence is a measure of how smart we are – or perhaps how smart we could be. Reality instead reflects how you apply who you are to the circumstances around you. Look at Peter and John in Acts 4:13.[24] The members of the Sanhedrin were amazed by their knowledge when the disciples spoke about God and Jesus. These doubting Sadducees knew Peter and John were ordinary men, yet they heard insightful speech. And these two men became extraordinary leaders, men who forged the future of Christianity, rallying thousands upon thousands to the cause of Christ.

As a Christian leader, you work to learn and gain wisdom. You practice and focus to convert wisdom quickly to understanding. You quickly apply wisdom and understanding to be effective in leading situations. Application of wisdom and understanding provides the revelation that is the right thing to do. *And* the power to do the right thing quickly.

Ask yourself these questions:

---

[24] Acts 4:13 *"Now when they saw the boldness of Peter and John, and perceived that they were uneducated, common men, they were astonished. And they recognized that they had been with Jesus."*

- Am I willing to learn from others, even if I perceive them to be less intelligent?
- Do I convert knowledge quickly into understanding and wisdom?
- Can I apply wisdom and understanding and act quickly in multiple circumstances?

Today, pray for intelligence.

Pray that the Holy Spirit will honor your hard work with wisdom and understanding. Pray James 3:13 that your behavior might reflect your wisdom and understanding. Confess your shortfalls and pray for improvement. Pray for intelligence in your leaders, pray for your followers to accept your wisdom as a strength, not a weakness. Pray God will present you with an opportunity to demonstrate your wisdom and knowledge. Pray that God will strengthen your faith so that you might grow in wisdom. Finally, thank God for your opportunities and praise Him for His leadership in your life.

DAY TWELVE
Imperative Two: Know the Right Thing To Do

PATIENCE

> "*Patience is the ability to accept delay, suffering, or annoyance without complaining or becoming angry.*"[25]

Biblical Reference: Ecclesiastes 7:8

> "*Better is the end of a thing than its beginning, and the patient in spirit is better than the proud in spirit.*"

"Joe" was developing a reputation. His peer line workers said while he was a good lineman, he was hard to find, despite his requirement to maintain radio contact and his well-defined work routine. Over and over again, I received complaints from people about calling Joe and getting no response. I talked to Joe about it, but he always had a good explanation. I needed to act but had no information. This was a serious situation that had the whole team questioning his reliability, and my ability to lead.

As the complaints mounted, my patience was running out. Joe continued to disappear and reappear, and I recruited a few people to help me track and record the instances. Rumors were flying about Joe, none of them helpful. The case was building, but still there was no real evidence to support any wrongdoing. Finally, a break after months of tracking,

---

[25] https://dictionary.cambridge.org/us/dictionary/english/patience

waiting, counseling sessions for Joe, and frustration for me. One of my recruits spotted Joe at a nearby apartment complex, right after he had turned up missing one day.

I grabbed my operations supervisor, and we drove out to the apartment and staked out Joe's company truck, parked out front. It didn't take long. Within a few minutes a man drove up and blocked the company truck with his vehicle. He grabbed a baseball bat and took off, running toward an apartment. Seconds later, we saw Joe, rolling out a back window of the apartment. Joe ran to his truck as the man continued to beat on the apartment door with his baseball bat. Joe began to move the truck out of the parking space with limited success, because the baseball-bat man's car was blocking his way. Finally, the man caught sight of the movement and left the apartment door. He zeroed in on Joe's company truck with the baseball bat and began to beat the truck. He destroyed the side-view mirror and was beginning to work on the driver's door. All the while Joe was inching his truck up and back, turning constantly to get around the blocking car.

About this time a young lady ran out of the apartment and draped herself over baseball-bat man. Joe couldn't take anymore and drove up over the curb and down through the grass to escape. He pulled out onto the highway; no doubt relieved to escape with only a few easily explained dents. Joe must have thought he was home-free until I pulled up behind him in my company car, called him on the radio, and ordered him to the office. After months of patience, I was finally able to deal with this issue that had plagued the team. This was Joe's last day of work for our company.

Strangely enough, I felt no release, no comfort in this accomplishment. Instead I felt a real burden to pray for Joe and his family. In time, I moved on, and Joe slipped out of my mind. Then came the Christmas card. I immediately noticed the return address and saw the card was from Joe. Inside was a beautiful answered prayer. After the incident, Joe found counseling and reconciled with his wife. In an earnest demonstration of Joe's true character, he put his life back on the right track. He could have easily veered down a different path. I found myself proud of the man, and the recovered life he had found.

Many years later Joe reached out to me again. He described a wonderful life, a new career and a great family. His children all with great jobs, contributing to society, with families of their own. As I look back today, I can see the real hero of this story. Not me, not Joe, but Joe's wife, Gloria. Gloria demonstrated more than patience, she demonstrated forbearance. When I think of forbearance, I think of biblical patience. That is patience in the face of difficulty. Her willingness and strength held this family together when most would have run away. Her behavior is a great example for leaders. Seek out patience when facing difficult circumstances. Be willing to look beyond the current situation at what could be, not just what is at the moment.

Patience challenges most leaders. Most of us focus on results, on speed of delivery, on action orientation. The last thing describing an active, engaged, and fast-moving leader is the word *patience*. However, patience is often what separates the best leaders from the rest of the pack. Patience is sometimes necessary to truly understand the right thing to do, such as with Joe's disappearances. Most of the time moving quickly, acting, or deciding quickly are good things. But from time to time, one needs to pause and reflect. Understanding when patience is needed provides an important key to good leadership, as is learning to apply patience properly.

For example, one must always be patient with people. This can be exhilarating, or it can be extraordinarily frustrating. Every person moves at his or her own individual speed. As a leader you must understand the capability of your team and push the members to their capability without pressing them beyond their competence. Every team has a slowest member. The leader's role is to understand if that person is slow or simply methodical. There are times when being methodical can be quite valuable, but slowness is seldom useful.

Once leaders understand their teams, leveraging the variable speed of the team becomes easier, maybe even automatic. But for new teams, or re-formed teams, a leader must take the time to understand how the different members operate. Only then can you assign tasks based on leveraging the individuals' skills, delegating those tasks that require speed to your fastest people and those tasks that require careful and methodical assembly to those whose skills lie in this area. One of the best skills of a leader is placing the square pegs in the square holes. You will also want to work with your people once you understand their skills. As you identify areas of weakness, look for opportunities to improve their individual and team skills.

Patience also requires that leaders develop an instinct to act or pause based on limited available knowledge. Again, this requires a rapid assessment of risk and results, often with incomplete information. How do you know when it is time to act or be patient? A savvy leader leverages experience to move as quickly as prudently possible, but willingly demonstrates patience when the risk of moving with incomplete information becomes higher than the perceived reward. As your experience grows, instinct follows.

Patience is a discipline more than a skill. We all have a degree of patience. Our personal discipline determines how we use it. Christians have a lot of experience with discipline. Failure of personal discipline leads the mature Christian to repentance. Repentance leads to grace, and grace leads to growth. The process of failure, repentance, and grace is a refinement process. With each failure and recovery, we grow stronger, more capable in areas of discipline. The Bible references this as the Refiner's Fire,[26] a process that strengthens the believer's faith and discipline. Patience is one of those disciplines refined through experience and time, leading to forbearance, that biblical level of patience, like that demonstrated by Joe's wife Gloria.

As a Christian leader, your demonstration of the discipline of patience becomes a part of your witness. Your patience couples with your other attributes to ensure you move appropriately when knowing the right direction to move. Patience doesn't make you slow; patience makes you competent. Even so, knowing when to demonstrate patience and when to demonstrate speed is a critical skill to master. The challenge is exerting patience when everyone is pushing for speed. Remember Ecclesiastes 7:8, the end is what you seek. Getting to the right end is far better than demonstrating speed toward the wrong end.

---

[26] Isaiah 48:10 *"Behold, I have refined you, but not as silver; I have tried you in the furnace of affliction."*;
Proverbs 17:3 *"The crucible is for silver, and the furnace is for gold, and the Lord tests hearts."*

Ask yourself these questions:

- Do I recognize times for patience?
- Do I have the discipline to call for a pause when everyone else is pushing forward?
- Does my relationship with God refine my ability to exercise discipline in all areas of my life?

Today, pray for patience.

Pray that the Holy Spirit will give you power over impatience. Pray Ecclesiastes 7:8 that you might keep your eyes on the end rather than the process. Confess your shortfalls and pray for improvement. Pray for patience in your leaders, pray for your followers to accept your patience as a strength, not a weakness. Pray God will present you with an opportunity to demonstrate effective patience. Pray that God will give you the discipline to master the appropriate balance between action and patience. Pray that you can overcome your desire to act when patience is the appropriate course. Finally, thank God for your opportunities and praise Him for His leadership in your life.

DAY THIRTEEN
Imperative Two: Know the Right Thing To Do

LISTENING

"Listening is to hear something with thoughtful attention."[27]

Biblical Reference: James 1:19

"Know this, my beloved brothers: let every person be quick to hear, slow to speak, slow to anger;"

In 2006, Duke Energy offered 9 billion dollars in stock to purchase the Cinergy Company of Cincinnati, Ohio. This was a good deal for both companies and the merger got underway quickly, but it didn't take long before the merger savings objectives began flowing downhill, rather than uphill. Soon, "Jim" from Cinergy and I were leading the Transmission and Distribution Merger to chase the formidable, cost-reduction targets that came with our new merger. We immediately assembled a team of knowledgeable, trustworthy people from both companies and started sorting through the complexities of putting the two cultures together.

One particularly difficult day, my friend Benny McPeak began to weave a complex story with an appropriately informative conclusion. I can no longer remember exactly what he said, but I remember he made excellent

---

[27] https://www.merriam-webster.com/dictionary/listen

simplification of one of our more difficult challenges. His synopsis helped push the team forward, which was a bit of a surprise to the Cinergy folks. They did not know Benny. He seemed the slow, easy-going Southerner, always talking about making things simple. In fact, he made sure people thought he was a simple man. Those who knew Benny understood that a sharp intellect and a way of making what was complex simple lay behind that ordinary exterior. That day, Benny took a complex problem and made it a simple problem. One of the Cinergy folks complimented him.

That's when Benny did something else for which he had a well-earned reputation. He said something mystifying, we called them "Benny-isms." For example, Benny sometimes had trouble spelling certain words, especially when he had to write on the board in front of a group. Instead of letting that bother him, he would always say, "It's a narrow-minded person who only spells a word one way." My all-time favorite Benny-ism occurred right after his outstanding synopsis in the Cinergy merger meeting. Benny finished up his comments, and the response went something like this.

Cinergy guy: "That is an excellent observation, Benny."

Benny: "What did I say, I wasn't listening!?"

Listening can be a challenge. Maybe a few folks are born with great listening skills, but most people work hard to listen. Oh, it's easy enough for most people to hear, but hearing and listening are two different skills. Just look at Solomon, who wrote Proverbs 12:15, *"The way of a fool is right in his own eyes, but a wise man listens to advice."* Solomon failed to listen to his own advice and found his way to failure by the end of his life. The same man who advises us to seek a spouse who fears the Lord[28] married 700 times, many times with pagan wives who ultimately drew him away from the Lord and lost him the Lord's favor.

Listening is an action verb. We hear with little to no attention. Listening is more difficult. Listening begins with hearing but also requires internalizing the message. To listen is to be actively engaged with the speaker: active eye contact and active verbal and physical acknowledgment—even follow-up questions to clarify understanding.

Unfortunately, most leaders fall into the trap of listening to the first couple of thoughts and then moving quickly to thinking of an impressive

---

[28] Proverbs 31:30 "Favor is deceitful, and beauty is vain: but a woman that fears the LORD, she shall be praised."

response. After all, as a leader, your selection came because of what you know, what you believe. I have a great deal of experience counting on my own knowledge over the thoughts of others. My personal fallback is to assume I always have the best answer. In fact, Benny once shared an example that caused me to rethink my default assumption.[29] Benny tells of an engineer in his team who always sat quietly, never offering ideas. Benny eventually determined to ask the man specifically for his opinion. He seldom spoke, but Benny soon realized that this quiet engineer often had the best idea in the room. Benny demonstrated active listening – at least for everyone but himself. That means working to listen to everyone, even the quietest one in the room. Benny's example demonstrates the danger of actively thinking of your response rather than engaging in active listening.

When you jump to thinking about your own response, you seldom improve that response; in fact, this often results in responses that are misaligned, improper, or even inappropriate. At the very least, it is obvious you weren't really listening. As a listener, you must trust your skills to give an extemporaneous response. As a professional leader, *listen* first, then *answer*. Become a professional listener. You're good enough not to prepare your response while others are speaking. Exercise active listening, like Benny describes, and both you and your team will benefit.

Listening also makes you and your team more capable. You might think of any challenge you have experienced. Opening the door to ideas beyond your own complements your style. Bob's idea to restore Huntsville's power helped me be a better leader. Considering the advice of others crafts a better solution and improves performance. Every individual has something to contribute. This is how God assembled the universe. He built us so together we compose a complex machine with billions of moving parts. Each part is important, each part has a purpose. By listening, you give each part an opportunity to fulfill his or her purpose in that moment. The result will be better answers to the challenges faced. The result will also be a demonstration of your personal understanding of God's plan, of God's Word, and of God's instruction for how we treat one another.

There are benefits of listening that directly relate to your testimony as a Christian. Consider 1 Peter 2:17, show respect to everyone.[29] When someone

---

[29] 1 Peter 2:17 (ESV) *"Honor everyone. Love the brotherhood. Fear God. Honor the emperor."*

is speaking, listening is a clear sign of respect. Even if you disagree, listen. As a Christian, and particularly as a Christian leader, people watch you to see the importance of the speaker's words. If you look away, if you check your cell phone, if you keep your eyes on your laptop, it becomes clear to everyone around you, as well as the speaker, that what this person says is unimportant. Peter says show respect to *everyone*. Engage and demonstrate to others that you are actively listening, and you convey respect. You demonstrate respect for the speaker, but you also demonstrate that you respect others. People will associate this respect with your leadership style, and as such, with your testimony as a Christian leader.

Listening creates a connection between the communicators, opening the door for deeper conversation. Just by listening actively, you and the speaker give each other permission to extend engagement. Perhaps, this is only necessary to explore areas of agreement, or options to consider. However, this may also create opportunities to speak more deeply about other topics, opening the door for spiritual conversations. Perhaps the speaker needs reassurance or support. Perhaps the speaker needs the gospel. By introducing a line of communication, you extend your testimony toward service. As people watch, you demonstrate approachability, humility, and compassion.

Finally, listening demonstrates God's love in your life. Through your willingness to listen you model Christ. This is an opportunity for Christian testimony without ever openly discussing Christ in a work environment. Listening is hard. Listening takes discipline. Listening takes maturity. But the benefits of listening are great. Listening shows respect, listening opens communication lines, and listening values each person's contribution. Listening is a picture of Matthew 7:12, "*do to others what you would have them do to you.*" When you listen, you become a channel for God's love and compassion in any and all settings.

Ask yourself these questions:

- Do I listen when others speak?
- Do I actively engage with speakers to let them know I am listening?
- Does how I listen truly reflect my testimony?

Today, pray for the ability to actively listen.

Pray that the Holy Spirit will help you pay attention, to keep you engaged. Pray James 1:19 that you might be quick to listen and slow to speak. Confess your shortfalls and pray for improvement. Pray for listening skills in your leaders, pray for your followers to see your listening as a testimony of God in your life. Pray God will present you with an opportunity to demonstrate your newfound attention to listening. Pray that God will strengthen your faith so you might listen as a reflection of God's love. Finally, thank God for your opportunities and praise Him for His leadership in your life.

DAY FOURTEEN
Imperative Two: Know the Right Thing To Do

SELF-AWARENESS

Self-awareness is "the knowledge and awareness of your own personality or character."[30]

Biblical Reference: 1 Timothy 4:16

"Keep a close watch on yourself and on the teaching. Persist in this, for by so doing you will save both yourself and your hearers."

People often challenge new leaders early, and this was certainly true for me as I moved in as Manager of Engineering, Construction, and Operations in the Charlotte Newell Office for Duke Power. The Newell group had a rebellious reputation, and I found the reputation well-earned. Two days after I arrived, one of my supervisors came in with a dilemma. He had driven up on a crew working an emergency. The crew had not properly grounded the wires, a fundamental error when working on energized or potentially energized wires. Poor grounding in the past resulted in serious issues, even death. As such, improper grounding egregiously violates the rules for every electric company.

But this was only the second day of my first week! I considered the

---

[30] http://www.learnersdictionary.com/definition/self-awareness

details of the grounding issue. I called in the crew and talked to them. The decision not to ground was not a clear decision in the minds of the crew. I listened to their explanation. I heard that one-time-in-one-hundred situation I described back when we were talking about doing the right thing. The rules clearly require grounding in all circumstances. The crew did not ground. This violates the rule. Yet, I understood the context of their decision after hearing them out. I did not fully agree with their assessment, but their description helped me see why they did not blindly follow the rules. These men felt grounding would have put them in more danger, because of the precarious nature of the work. When they arrived, there was a car stuck up against the pole, two poles were down, and wires were crisscrossing over one another. In their opinion, grounding would require first sorting out all the wires, and they did not see this as necessary or easy to complete. They were adamant that grounding was not appropriate.

Their description encouraged me to lobby on their behalf for a reduced penalty. Their new supervisor was just as adamant that grounding was necessary and lobbied for a heavy penalty. This left me with a judgment call. Do I support their supervisor, or do I support the crew? I talked with my new boss, the Charlotte Regional Manager. He wanted to fire them. Considering the situation, I felt there was a pretty good chance their judgment had some merit. In the end, I avoided more egregious punishment and we decided to give them a written reprimand, a lighter penalty considering the issue.

My boss and their immediate supervisor felt this punishment was too light. Essentially this was an escalated warning that positioned them for termination should any additional violations occur. I felt pretty good that I had considered all the angles and found a middle ground that left us in a good place. In the end, all agreed it was a reasonable compromise. I sorted out the right thing to do. The men, true to their reputation, posted their confidential written reprimands on the Union bulletin board in the locker room for all to see. The "Union" board was a free space for the men. The International Brotherhood of Electrical Workers (IBEW) represented the line workers. One of the agreements between the Union and the company was a space for workers to post grievances and communications. What should have been a confidential conversation between the men and me became a public discussion point.

This first week was busy, and I was multi-tasking. One task was readying my new office. Running a computer cable would finish up all I needed before moving in. I tired of waiting for facilities people, my impatience took over, and I decided to do the work myself. I found a step ladder and started work. My ladder was a little short, but I was able to get the job done by standing on the top step of the ladder with my head through the ceiling. It was a simple matter. I threw the new cable as far as I could, then crawled up to the top step of the ladder again and threw it some more. In just a few tries, I had a cable run through the drop-down ceiling from my new office back to the central console. I was proud of getting the job done and settled into my new office with now three days behind me, and my computer working perfectly.

On day four, I came into the office and found a letter on my desk. The letter was an exact copy of the written reprimand I had given the men. Except my name was on the letter, instead of theirs. Ladder safety was in the area where I had described the grounding violation. The men had given me a written reprimand for ladder safety! They were absolutely right. I violated the rules. I knew about ladder safety rules but didn't really think about applying them personally. I was in charge; therefore, I was able to use my own judgment about the safety of the situation. I considered my own judgment higher than those of the men working an emergency.

This was a wake-up call. A failure in self-awareness. A reminder that someone is always watching, a lesson I repeated later at TVA when the young lady called me out for leaving work early every day. A failure in leadership during my first four days. I went back to the locker room and pinned my letter up beside theirs on the union bulletin board. Later, the guys would tell me that was when they knew I would be a good boss. They were concerned how I might react, and some were worried I might call them back in for more punishment.

Being self-aware is a trap for leaders at all levels. Growth in responsibility and power over others inevitably leads us to increasing comfort when executing that same responsibility and power. We begin to discard the input of others as unnecessary. After all, we wouldn't be in charge if we didn't deserve to be in charge, right? As confidence and experience grows, many times with successful outcomes, we tend to listen more to ourselves, and less to others. The more successful we are, the less likely we are to look beyond ourselves.

Self-awareness can be counterintuitive to action-based, confident leadership. Leaders act with purpose and resolve. Often acting quickly, guiding others to successful conclusions by their insight and actions. Yet there always comes a time in leaders' experience where their inability to see beyond their own perspectives leads teams into unfortunate circumstances. Historical examples exist in droves of leaders who failed because they believed in their own greatness. Consider Alexander the Great, whose empire splintered on his death, because he refused to name a successor. Or Julius Caesar, who never saw the alienation of the Senate before they attacked and killed him. Or Adolf Hitler's inwardly focused, neurotic decision-making as World War II began to unravel for the Germans. Leaders who fail majestically as they lose their self-awareness riddle the history books.

It is truly impossible to consistently discern the right thing if you are unable to look beyond yourself. No one gets everything right, every time. Paul's words to Timothy are priceless to any leader: *"Keep a close watch on yourself."*[31] Treat yourself as your own sub-ordinate. Analyze and think through your actions. When there is time, do this as you make decisions and take actions. If there is no time, make sure you do an after-action review. When you speak to a group, ask yourself afterward about the perception you gave. Find a few trusted folks and ask them how you can do better. When you take actions, review those actions first with yourself, then with your trust group. Look for insights into things you had not considered. Write down what you learn so you can improve next time. Remember always that you are not above the rules of the people you serve as leader.

Self-awareness requires constant attention. This is why Paul advised Timothy to keep watch in 1 Timothy 4:16. Paul knew the early church would face terrible persecution, and he was encouraging Timothy to hold fast to his beliefs and practices. Paul understood how church leaders would have to keep their eyes on Jesus or the challenges might overwhelm them. Even the best leaders get overconfident and depend on their own abilities

---

[31] 1 Timothy 4:16

to the detriment of the team. They lose sight of the big picture. The advantage Christians have here is prayer and perspective. We can pray for the Holy Spirit to open our eyes to self-awareness. We can leverage the perspective of a great and powerful God, a loving God willing to sacrifice His own son. This perspective is humbling and reminds us that we are never as great as we might think we are. Romans 3:23 reminds that we *all* sin.[32] We *all* fall short of God's glory. As a Christian leader, lead with the perspective that you can always be better.

Ask yourself these questions:

- Am I aware of how my actions impact others?
- Do I pray for self-awareness when I pray for confidence?
- Do I seek feedback to improve my self-awareness?

Today, pray for self-awareness.

Pray that the Holy Spirit maintains your self-awareness. Pray 1 Timothy 4:16 that you might keep watch over yourself in all things. Confess your shortfalls and pray for improvement. Pray for self-awareness in your leaders, pray for your followers to help you and keep you on track by offering constructive feedback. Pray God will present you with an opportunity to demonstrate self-awareness. Pray that God will strengthen your faith so that you grow comfortable when questioned, even by yourself. Finally, thank God for your opportunities and praise Him for His leadership in your life.

---

[32] Romans 3:23: "*for all have sinned and fall short of the glory of God,*"

DAY FIFTEEN
Imperative Two: Know the Right Thing To Do

PROBLEM SOLVING

Problem solving is "the process or act of finding a solution to a problem or issue."[33]

Biblical Reference: Philippians 4:6

"Do not be anxious about anything, but in everything by prayer and supplication with thanksgiving let your requests be made known to God."

Growing up on a farm often develops problem-solving skills early and extensively. Our access to repair parts or components is unlikely, which results in improvisation. My father taught me improvisation many years ago. He had an uncanny ability to find a way to make anything work. He once bought several boxes of parts from the local Honda dealer and assembled two Mopeds. Never mind that one ran backwards when it first started! That same ingenuity led to cutting the back off a Chevy Vega, replacing it with a homemade, wooden truck body and making a one-of-a-kind Vega truck. Or better still, welding together a chopped-down Cadillac hearse and a rusty old van dragged from a hog pen to make a unique hearse camper. When a need existed, a solution was always nearby.

---

[33] https://www.merriam-webster.com/dictionary/problem-solving

Most kids in Farm Life where I grew up learned problem solving while working in tobacco. Tobacco is a challenging product to bring to market. Harvesting tobacco happens only once the tobacco is ready and we could pull the tobacco leaves in the field, loop them on sticks, and hang them in the barn for curing. Then my uncle's workers would remove those cured tobacco sticks from the barn and gather them as loose tobacco leaves for sale. The process is time consuming and labor intensive. I loved my time driving the harvester tractor, but the time came for me to advance beyond the new kid, tractor driver. I moved up to hanging tobacco, a job I mentioned earlier.

Tobacco barns are about the size of a small, tall house, maybe three stories. They hold about 600 to 800 sticks of looped tobacco, hung on "tier poles." Tier poles, normally old de-barked trees, run horizontally across the barn, about four feet apart, just wide enough that a stick of tobacco could hang between the poles. They were often smooth, and my cousins and I hung tobacco with bare feet to grip the poles better. The sticks hung across between two tier poles, with the leaves draping below the stick. The barns are high, and the poles stack up one above another so multiple levels of tobacco sticks can be cured at one time. Tier poles stack up five, six, even seven sections high, right up against the angled roofline.

For some reason, we called the top-tier poles in the barn the "wind-beams." I never figured out why. There is absolutely *no* wind blowing on a ninety-degree day in the top of a tin-roofed barn! (Years later in Civil Engineering class I would learn wind-beams is an architectural term.) Hanging the wind beams meant hanging the top. I often started with the wind beams early in the morning before it got too hot. Hanging the wind beams is the toughest part in the barn. Getting it done first was important on hot days.

If you're having trouble visualizing a tobacco barn, think of a giant chest-of-drawers, without the drawers. Instead of drawers, four-and-a-half-foot wide sticks loaded with tobacco hung, one after another. First the top "drawer." Then the next and so on until the chest is completely filled with tobacco sticks.

Tobacco sticks are gnarled pieces of old wood, just long enough to span the space between the tier poles, about four feet or so. As you saw in my earlier description of my first day at work in the tobacco fields, the loopers loaded these tobacco sticks in the field. Then the lead farmer (Uncle Zack) stacked them on a pallet. The pallets then moved to the barn to be loaded one at a time into the barn for curing. Hanging sticks in the barn meant I would scramble up and down the tier poles, moving and hanging the individual sticks on the way to a full barn. Up at the top of the barn in the wind beams, I would end up about forty feet off the ground, straddling the four-foot gap between the tier poles!

The constant moving up and down the tiers made hanging a young man's job. Straddling two poles as I hung twenty-five-pound sticks of tobacco a few inches apart all day was hard work. We usually hung with three workers, all in their teens. One unloaded the pallets, bringing sticks of tobacco in the barn and handing up as high as he could to the bottom hanger about seven-or-eight feet above the dirt floor. The bottom hanger was the one with the greatest reach, the tallest. For my team of younger cousin hangers, this was normally me. I would straddle the bottom set of tier poles and hang what I could reach, normally three rows higher, maybe eight-or-nine feet. After that, I would pass the sticks up to the top hanger, who stood on the third pole up. He would hang about three more poles high, then park several sticks as high as he could reach. This top man would scramble up higher to the wind beams and move the parked sticks into their curing position. This process slowly filled the barn, top to bottom.

Sometimes we ended up short one person. That meant either my cousin or I hung both the bottom and the top of the barn. I would scramble up to the top, then go back down, handling many of the sticks multiple times as I moved them up in stages, often between pallet loads of tobacco sticks. This was an exhausting and slow job.

My uncle thought perhaps a technological solution might resolve this problem for us, and also potentially reduce his labor costs. He purchased a device called a "save-a-man." The save-a-man was a geared, motor-driven lift, with the ability to raise multiple loaded tobacco sticks up into the barn. We couldn't wait to try it.

The save-a-man was a disaster!

This device weighed about eighty pounds, which is a tough load for a thirteen-year-old or fourteen-year-old straddling a four-foot space in bare feet. My cousins and I struggled to hang the machine in place on the bottom tier pole about seven-or-eight feet high. Save-a-man seemed well-designed on the surface. Think of it as a vertical conveyor belt. A little wider than a tobacco stick, chain driven with hooks spaced every couple of feet where we could hang a stick while standing on the ground.

To make the system work with one less worker, we needed to move the top of the conveyor up to the third-or-fourth tier pole high, after we initially hung it on the bottom tier. That put the top of the conveyor about fifteen-to-twenty feet up in the barn, hung over a tier pole. My cousin and I climbed up and man-handled the device up one tier at a time, until we managed to hang it on the third-or-fourth tier. Because there were only two of us hanging on these days, my cousin and I moved the save-a-man in small increments as we began to fill the barn. It took both of us to move it each time. The result? A ground worker could hang a stick on the bottom hooks of the save-a-man, and the conveyor would lift the stick up to the fourth tier, essentially replacing the bottom hanger.

But if you were hanging up on the top, you would find a stick rising up from the ground to meet you every few seconds. The save-a-man came with a limit switch on top, which was supposed to stop the chain-driven lift as a stick reached the top. Within a few minutes the limit switch broke completely off. Because the save-a-man was so heavy, I didn't want to move it. So, we parked the save-a-man in the middle of the barn, and I ran back and forth all through the top of the barn, throwing sticks into their spots as quickly as possible. If I was scrambling a few tier poles over to hang a stick, I struggled to get back before the next stick reached the top.

The lack of a top limit switch inevitably led to the save-a-man demonstrably flinging a full stick of tobacco off the top, dropping it twenty feet or so to the ground, often on top of the person loading the bottom of the lift! This drop destroyed the careful looping and required re-looping the stick. For the first several hours, the process took twice as long, and twice as many people to hang tobacco.

We renamed the device "lose-a-man."

However, as the day wore on, we found a rhythm and solved the problems with the machine. We began loading every four feet rather than the two feet between the hooks mounted on the conveyor. Using space between positions provided more time between tobacco sticks. We moved the heavy "lose-a-man" once per section, requiring a little less back and forth, up and down as we hung the sticks. In the end, the machine worked effectively.

We determined that if we were one person short, we could use lose-a-man to replace that person. However, the whole process was exhausting and required about twice the effort. In the end, the solution wasn't big enough for the problem, and we threw the lose-a-man out in the woods for another day. The extra farm hand was far more effective, and cheaper as well! Last I saw, my uncle had removed the lose-a-man motor and put it to use solving a different problem.

Leading is all about problem solving, since problems land in the laps of leaders. The problem may be employees requiring attention, or issues needing resolution, or systems that don't work as they should. No matter the problem, people turn to leaders for solutions, which come in many different flavors. Some demand the detailed, carefully planned approach. Others may resolve with minimal information, using your experiences to weave possible answers. One thing is sure, if you lead, you will face problems that require solutions. If you want to know what the right thing is in any circumstance, problem solving is a skill that requires mastery.

We learn to solve problems from an early age. In the beginning, our problem is about getting something to eat or getting out of a crib. The skills we learn even then are the same skills we use years later, like good behavior equals reward, or work leads to more freedom. As we grow, our experience leads to knowledge, which we use to solve more and more complex problems. I could never have dealt effectively with "Jennifer" had I not already experienced firing "Joe." The experience of dealing with rules and regulations of terminating employment helped me soften the impact with Jennifer. Experience brought internalized knowledge, which helped me do the right thing. Doing the right thing largely depends on the problem. If the problem is complex and the implications of solutions are highly impactful, careful consideration is due. However, solving a simple problem with light impact may only rely on personal experience and knowledge, without additional digging.

When facing a problem, first consider the implications of being incorrect. This is almost as important as solving the problem itself. Ask your peers, your boss, or even your employees if the outcome is not obvious. Once you understand the risk, you can determine the level of caution and care taken to develop solutions. Again, solution development can be a group activity, or you may do it alone if you have enough information and experience. Finally, the consideration of speed is also important. Is it important to solve this issue immediately or do I have time to consider other options?

The secret to effective problem-solving is finding the right-size solution for the problem at hand. As the problem grows, the solution may need to also grow. For simple problems, often a simple solution is best, like skipping a position on lose-a-man. Once in a while, even complex problems have simple solutions, but more often they require complex thought to reach the right answer.

The Christian leader understands solving problems, since the Bible is full of mankind's problems. And the Christian leader understands the role God is willing to play in helping us solve problems. Consider Proverbs 3: 6, *"In all your ways acknowledge him, and he will make straight your paths."* Problem solving is most often about straightening a crooked pathway. Prayer helps. After all, *"Ask, and it will be given to you."*[34] As a Christian leader, ask. Pray about your problems. Be open to how God uses the people around you to bring you answers. Listen, watch, learn, and be bold. You may not always like the answers God brings, but He always delivers an answer.

Basically, learn to trust the Lord!

Ask yourself these questions:

- Am I willing to listen to others when seeking solutions to problems?
- Do I pray for solutions?
- Am I bold in offering answers to challenging problems?

Today, pray for your own personal, problem-solving ability.

Pray that the Holy Spirit will fill your mind with the right options to consider. Pray Philippians 4:6 that you "will not be anxious" and that you will "let your requests be known to God." Confess your shortfalls and pray for improvement. Pray for problem-solving ability in your leaders, pray for your followers to offer

---

[34] Matthew 7:7

suggestions and demonstrate discernment in solution development. Pray God will present you with an opportunity to demonstrate your willingness to help solve problems. Pray that God will strengthen your faith so that you might grow in this area. Finally, thank God for your opportunities and praise Him for His leadership in your life.

DAY SIXTEEN
Imperative Two: Know the Right Thing To Do

DISCERNMENT

> *"Discernment is the ability to judge people and things well."*[35]

Biblical Reference: 1 Corinthians 2:14

> *"The person without the Spirit does not accept the things that come from the Spirit of God but considers them foolishness and cannot understand them because they are discerned only through the Spirit."*

In early 2000 my family faced a difficult choice. Duke Power purchased Pan Energy and became Duke Energy. Duke sought leaders to exchange between companies, and my first vice president offer came my way, in Texas. I was not excited about leaving home and moving to Texas. My wife had a great job that she loved, one daughter was at NC State and two were in high school. Texas meant leaving everything behind and starting over in Houston.

I prayed over and over for an obvious answer, yet God seemed quiet. I know and understand Matthew 6:25, *"Therefore I tell you, do not be anxious about your life, what you will eat or what you will drink, nor about*

---

[35] https://dictionary.cambridge.org/us/dictionary/english/discernment

your body, what you will put on. Is not life more than food, and the body more than clothing?"

I believe God's provision for me is greater than my own personal idea of my provision. I was certainly not seeking prosperity; I really just wanted to trust God to lead me in the right direction. I needed help. I wanted to be in His will. Was Houston in God's will? Was Houston my own pride and desire to move up? I wanted so much to do the right thing, but I just could not see the right thing in this situation.

I fell back on my engineering instincts and like all engineers, I made a spreadsheet. In the spreadsheet I listed twenty-one conditions that I needed the Houston folks to meet. Most of these were pretty easy: salary, bonus structure, vacation, and so forth. Only a couple were challenging, like a house purchase plan, a signing bonus, and extended, temporary living arrangements. In addition to meeting spreadsheet conditions, I wanted to talk face to face with a friend and mentor, Benny (of the Benny-isms). But Benny McPeak had taken a job in far western North Carolina, about three hours away. Finally, if I was going to leave Duke Power, I wanted to speak with the Duke Power president to be sure this was a good idea for my career, and just maybe secure a later pathway back to Charlotte and the comforts of Duke. After praying for so long, it felt good to act, to grab ownership of the decision. In other words, if God wasn't going to answer me, I would work it out for myself. Then there came the inevitable "But God" moment.

One morning I was reviewing my decision spreadsheet when my perspective new boss from Houston called. One by one, he reviewed my conditions, and met all twenty-one, even the house purchase plan, signing bonus, and extended, temporary living arrangements. My plan was working, I was checking off all the boxes on the way to a decision. Then, within a few minutes, I was shocked when Benny McPeak knocked on my office door. He had traveled to Charlotte for a meeting and had an hour to kill before that meeting. He asked me how things were going, and I invited him to sit and talk.

That same evening, I attended a reception of some two thousand folks, and as I was standing in the middle of the crowd, I felt a tap on my shoulder. The president of Duke Power was standing there behind me. He asked if he could speak with me and reassure me of the pending decision. Some people see all this as coincidence, or maybe fate, or perhaps a remarkable plan. I tend to think of such occurrences as God's way of grabbing our attention.

These "coincidences" were the Holy Spirit showing me God's will in my life. Desperate for an answer, I had made my own plan. But God used a baseball bat (like Joe's adversary) and hit me on the head with it. You would have to be blind not to discern God had a plan for our family in Houston, no matter how difficult it would be. I thought I had a great plan, but God had a plan for my family all along. I thought I had to figure this out for myself, while all the time, God was making me think through what the decision really meant. He was teaching me discernment and gave me this wonderful "Aha" moment to demonstrate His providence and guidance on our lives.

There are times when knowing the right thing to do seems impossible. At these times every choice often looks like a bad choice, with no good options available. There are also times when you need a decision, but no good pathway is clear. When faced with no obvious answer, Christians have an obvious solution. Turn to God and pray for discernment. Maybe you will experience "coincidences" or more and more information that leads to a decision. Discernment seldom describes worldly leaders. Yet when you are unsure of your pathway, discernment is critical. Mature Christians understand discernment as a gift of God, listed among the spiritual gifts in 1 Corinthians 12.[36] According to the Bible, discernment is the ability to identify false teaching. Discernment also describes the ability to size up a person or circumstance through the Holy Spirit's guidance.

Discernment is not easy. Before God gave me the answer to Houston, I studied and analyzed the options. Building knowledge and understanding about circumstances and issues serves as an enabler for discernment. The more you understand, the more the right decision becomes apparent. Even so, not all decisions are easily discernable. Even the most discerning Christian faces the unknown from time to time. When you clearly don't know what is right, ask for help. When necessary, make your best assessment given your moral and spiritual judgment. Discernment is 80 percent listening to God and the Holy Spirit. The other 20 percent requires

---

[36] 1 Corinthians 12:8: *"For to one is given through the Spirit the utterance of wisdom, and to another the utterance of knowledge according to the same Spirit,"*

individual hard work and the willingness to boldly make decisions based on experience and your faith.

Ask yourself these questions:

- When facing a difficult decision, do I often ask God for help?
- Do I wait for God to answer through the Holy Spirit or move without an answer?
- Do I prepare and analyze options before moving ahead with decisions?

Today, pray for discernment.

Pray that the Holy Spirit will help you see the right answer in all circumstances. Pray 1 Corinthians 2:14 that you might look for the Lord's guidance. Confess your shortfalls and pray for improvement. Pray for discernment in your leaders, pray for your followers to trust your guidance and believe in your ability to discern. Pray God will present you with an opportunity to experience discernment. Pray that God will strengthen your faith that you might grow in discernment. Finally, thank God for your opportunities and praise Him for His leadership in your life.

DAY SEVENTEEN
IMPERATIVE TWO: KNOW THE RIGHT THING TO DO

PERSPECTIVE

> *"Perspective is the capacity to view things in their true relations or relative importance."*[37]

Biblical Reference: Isaiah 46:10 (NIV)

> *"I make known the end from the beginning, from ancient times, what is still to come. I say, 'My purpose will stand, and I will do all that I please.'"*

I had been in Houston only a couple of years when it happened. In 2003, my Boston-based team began a six-month, pipeline project, which I rank as my greatest professional failure. The project was unbelievable, the most difficult ever attempted by our company. Yet our charge seemed simple: Connect only a few miles of pipe. We were to join the Maritimes and Northeast Pipeline system in Salem, Massachusetts, with the Texas Eastern System, just south of Boston, a total of about twenty-one miles. The routing through this heavily congested area was complicated, involving seven horizontal directional drills (HDD's). An HDD was a laser-guided drill that operated sideways and created a tunnel. In this tunnel you pump something called drilling mud, which hardened along the sides. Once

---

[37] https://www.merriam-webster.com/dictionary/perspective

complete, you simply pulled in a new pipe through the tunnel. We had HDD's under golf courses and under an interstate. We had HDD's from shore to offshore, from offshore to offshore, and from offshore to onshore. We even had an HDD under the runway at Boston's Logan Airport!

Once offshore, the pipeline would be ten feet underground in the Boston harbor, then covered in concrete to prevent damage from anchoring ships. This became a complex project, because of the many different components. We ran pipe from the end of the Maritimes and Northeast pipeline through downtown Salem, Massachusetts, crossing under the interstate, building through the busy Boston harbor, drilling forty feet below the ground level of Logan Airport (because the last airplane crash there dug a thirty-foot hole). Then back onshore through a busy industrial park to join with the Texas Eastern pipe. All in all, each component of the project seemed feasible. We had done work like this before, just never all at once. We looked at each individual task and concluded we could do the job for the target price necessary to make a viable project.

Unfortunately, there were delays from the beginning. First, we had to hold public hearings and site the project. No one wants a pipeline in their yard, and as you might expect, this was a major battle until we finally secured a site. Once we had a siting plan, we needed a permit from the federal government to build an interstate pipeline, because we connected two interstate pipelines. The permitting lasted much longer than expected. Instead of starting in the spring as we had planned, we started in late fall. This late start time meant we were going to build this daunting project in the Boston winter of 2003, one of the worst winters in history.

The harbor froze solid.

We hired an icebreaker to go in front of the pipeline barge. The project required divers to position the pipe and feed the concrete at the bottom of the harbor. The divers refused to work, because they could not find a way to surface with all the ice above them. At one point we had enough vessels on the frozen harbor to rack up 1 million dollars a day. And the divers were not working! On the final HDD we began losing drilling mud as we came back onshore from the harbor. Apparently, the tides had created caverns in the ocean floor, and we were filling them with mud. We had pumped gallon after gallon of drilling mud into the ground, and all that mud just seemed to disappear. Finally, mud broke out of the ground and filled a security shack, with the security man inside! You can imagine that he was not a happy man.

A nearby water tower collapsed!

The considerable underground action from the pressure of the missing mud led to a crack in a water tower, which was holding wastewater. Within a couple days, the tower collapsed. We had just enough time to pump the wastewater into a disposal barge before the tower came down.

Local lobstermen railed at us.

Our thirty-inch pipe on the floor of Boston harbor blocked the migration of lobsters, halting the mating cycle and leading to a dry year for lobster fishing in Boston.

The most complex project ever attempted was far more complex than we ever imagined. Yet we finished the job, and gas is now flowing through this pipeline. Cost? Almost twice the original estimate! A terrible performance for a new vice president. I should have known it. We looked at each complex component as an individual project. One by one, we could have completed any of those components with ease. However, grouped together, the complexities multiplied. This was an impossible task. I should have added a contingency plan to each component and another contingency plan to the overall project. Instead we squeezed the contingency to make the numbers work. They didn't work at all. This was a failure to get the big picture. Instead of gaining perspective over the whole project, I broke it down, and looked one by one at each component. There was so much I got wrong during this six-month project.

Gaining perspective over the entire work is one of the most important things you must do as a leader. In Boston, I was one of the guys. I worked alongside the crews. I was there day in and day out in the frigid temperatures. I lost track of the big picture, because the little pictures were so compelling.

It is possible to know what is right without having the big picture. However, that knowledge will certainly be fleeting. If you lead, you must see beyond the moment. If you lead, you must understand what may be around the corner, such as the ice in Boston harbor. If you intend to be a good leader, you must find a way to gain perspective beyond the minutia of the day to day and get a bigger picture of what is happening. This can be very difficult if you are close to your organization, or if you enjoy working alongside your people as I was in that freezing weather. The closer you are to the day-to-day work, the more difficult to see over the horizon.

There is no real secret to having perspective beyond the day to day. This is not a skill so much as a discipline. As a leader you must condition yourself to always see beyond your own circumstances. If you want to be a candidate for the next, higher leadership position, you must lead as if you are already in that position. For example, many leaders strive with great passion and engagement to achieve team goals. Yet time and again, achievement of team goals comes at the cost of broader organizational goals. In other words, teams often optimize their own performance at the expense of other parts of the organization. Leaders cannot lose track of the broader responsibilities of the larger organization. Leaders need to find a way to achieve team goals without hurting others to get there. By increasing perspective, leaders help redirect teams that are off track or encourage teams that are on track.

As individuals we are always part of something greater than ourselves. Always trying to look at things from a higher perspective seems simple enough. Unfortunately, gaining perspective is very challenging. This is particularly true when you are deeply involved in complex and difficult work.

This is also true of our spiritual lives, isn't it? How often do we become focused intently on what is happening right now in our lives? We lose track of the bigger picture. Sometimes we find ourselves mired in bad times. It feels as if the bad times will never end.

But God is always there. God always sees the bigger picture. As Isaiah tells us in 46:10, God already knows the end. He knows how things turn out. It takes discipline for us to manage our spiritual lives to see beyond the here and now. This same discipline enables us to see above our current circumstances in all things.

Climb up. Find a way to gain God's perspective. This positions you far better for discovering the right thing to do.

Ask yourself these questions:

- Am I enamored with day-to-day details?
- Am I able to gain perspective over my current circumstances?
- Do I lead, or do I prefer to work alongside?

Today, pray for perspective.

Pray that the Holy Spirit will give you the discipline to rise above the day-to-day details of life. Pray Isaiah 46:10 that you might trust the Lord to show you the end, guiding you as you broaden your perspective. Confess your shortfalls and pray for improvement. Pray for perspective in your leaders, pray for your followers to understand and acknowledge when you are looking beyond today's challenge. Pray God will present you with an opportunity to demonstrate perspective. Pray that God will strengthen your discipline so you might routinely gain the perspective you need, both in your job and in your spiritual life. Finally, thank God for your opportunities and praise Him for His leadership in your life.

DAY EIGHTEEN
Imperative Two: Know The Right Thing To Do

CALM

"Calm is a state in which you are not affected by strong emotions such as excitement, anger, shock, or fear."[38]

Biblical Reference: Philippians 4:6-7

"Do not be anxious about anything, but in everything by prayer and supplication with thanksgiving let your requests be made known to God. And the peace of God, which surpasses all understanding, will guard your hearts and your minds in Christ Jesus."

Hurricane Hugo behaved badly. In 1989 hurricane forecasting lacked the accuracy of today. Hugo roared into Charleston, South Carolina, with 150 mph winds and rapidly ran inland on a northwestern track, predicted to head straight toward Raleigh. At Duke Power we braced for hurricane winds along the eastern border of our territory and had already begun to shift crews from Charlotte east toward Raleigh. We braced ourselves as we prepared for the forecasted path.

But Hugo refused to cooperate. Instead of tracking eastward, Hugo continued inland and pierced the city of Charlotte about 4 A.M. I woke

---

[38] https://www.macmillandictionary.com/us/dictionary/american/calm_3

up to a roar unlike anything I had ever heard as hurricane winds lashed the night. As our power went out, I immediately headed to work. This day would be the first of many twenty, twenty-four, and even thirty-hour days. When Hugo finally moved out of town, not a single Newell customer we served had power. Not one shining light early that morning.

Hugo was a crisis.

The entire first day crews cleared trees from the roads and then made their way back to the Operations Center. There was no hope of bringing in help from outside our area; we were on our own for those early days of recovery. Hyped up on coffee and Diet Coke we laid out our strategy and got to work. For me personally, this was my first real opportunity to bond with my rambunctious new team. Only six months earlier I had moved to take over the northwest quadrant of Charlotte. This was my first test as the leader. I knew it and the workers did as well.

There were many opportunities to lose my composure in the first few days. Eventually we began to see help arrive from out-of-town. On one occasion my out-of-towners managed to alienate an entire hotel staff! We got the call mid-day to remove all 300 men and women from the hotel. Despite our protests, the hotel management would not change their mind. All the crews were working, so we did the only thing we could. We sent over a group of folks to load pickup trucks with luggage and other personal items strewn around 150 rooms. We either did that or the hotel would put their belongings in a pile in the parking lot. Our folks assembled those belongings as best they could and brought them back to the Operations Center.

Then we found everyone new rooms. Our crew came in about 9 P.M. from a sixteen-hour workday. They found their personal items stacked in a conference room, mixed in with their roommate's possessions. One guy seemed more irritated than any of the others. He may have been the biggest guy I ever saw doing line work. He unloaded his emotions on one of the young women who had gotten the belongings, and everyone heard it. As the crowd gathered, it was my time at bat.

I remember thinking, *This is a leadership moment. This is why all these people are watching. They think this big guy is going to let the new boss have it.* As I walked over to this man, I asked God to calm my spirit and guide my words. I don't know if the Holy Spirit took over, or if just talking to God calmed me, but I faced the guy with the most confidence I had felt since arriving six months earlier. I talked quietly and calmly to the large man, apologized for what had happened and explained why we had to do what we did. I also suggested that his language and the loudness of his voice—while understandable given the circumstances—was about to get him sent back to wherever he came from. I suggested he might choose his next words carefully and asked him if he had any questions.

He had only one question. "Where is my new hotel located?" Then he thanked me for the explanation and apologized to the young lady. Rational people almost always react calmly when faced calmly. From this point forward, the Newell people would do anything for me. By the way, I would have done anything for them as well. We took four weeks to rebuild the system. But it only took a moment to forge a leadership bond with these wonderful men and women.

That moment always comes back to me when I read Isaiah 41:10 *"Fear not, for I am with you; be not dismayed, for I am your God; I will strengthen you, I will help you, I will uphold you with my righteous right hand."*

Crisis moments come to all of us. There are times in every life when we come face to face with a crisis. Crises are never fun, and they often shape the rest of our lives. Events like job loss or the death of a spouse, a parent, or a child change us all. The crises we face remind us that we do not live in paradise. Our world is under the judgment of sin, and this can be a tremendously difficult world.

Yet God equips us to deal effectively with a crisis. *"For God gave us a spirit not of fear but of power and love and self-control."*[39] Sometimes our crisis belongs to us, alone. Cancer, job loss, financial troubles all reflect inwardly. These kinds of crisis require a trusting relationship with God and a supportive group of believing friends and family. But sometimes a crisis is a group effort, like the Hugo Hurricane. In these times leadership rises. A leader's strength is never more evident than in the midst of a crisis. The best leader brings passion and intensity to the challenge yet keeps his or her emotions under control. The best leader exudes a sense of calm competence, no matter the difficulties.

As a Christian leader, you have a resource to call upon when you face a crisis. God is ready to hold you in His righteous right hand. If you are reacting poorly, if you find yourself becoming overly excited or afraid,

---

[39] 2 Timothy 1:7

then you are outside of God's will. God tells us to fear not. Jesus Himself provides the best example as He stands silent before the Sanhedrin, facing certain and painful death on the cross. If Jesus can face crucifixion without fear, can you not also face the crisis before you? After all, there is always something beyond the crisis, often a good result like the bond between me and the Newell men and women.

People search for those folks who manage to stay calm, no matter what they face. This is true leadership. When you are calm, you think more clearly, you make better decisions, you have greater confidence. When you are calm, you can better identify the right thing to do. When you are calm, people around you will notice, and their own agitation eases. If you are the kind of person who gets anxious easily, pray and ask God to help you with your anxiety. If you know a crisis is coming, tell yourself to stay calm and remind yourself when the crisis arrives. If you feel anxiety, stop and pray. It doesn't matter if people see you; in fact, you may strengthen your witness if they do.

God wants to hold you in His righteous right hand, but He is waiting for you to ask.

Ask yourself these questions:

- Do I allow anxiety to drive my behavior?
- Am I willing to pause in a crisis long enough to ask God for help?
- Can I be bold enough to claim God's promise and seek His right hand in the midst of a crisis?

Today, pray for power over anxiety.

Pray that the Holy Spirit will keep you calm in difficult circumstances. Pray Philippians 4:6-7 that you might trust God to help you through crisis situations. Confess your shortfalls and pray for improvement. Pray for calmness in your leaders, pray for your workers to follow your lead and remain calm when facing challenging issues. Pray God will present you with an opportunity to demonstrate power over anxiety. Pray that God will help you to "not be anxious in anything," but have a spirit of control that results in your being calm in a crisis. Finally, thank God for your opportunities and praise Him for His leadership in your life.

DAY NINETEEN
Imperative Three: Find Joy in All You Do

Biblical Reference: James 1:2-3

> *"Consider it pure joy, my brothers and sisters, whenever you face trials of many kinds, because you know that the testing of your faith produces perseverance."*

I learned about the pure joy of work first on the tobacco field over fifty years ago. Every year, we looked forward to one day over all the others. There was nothing like "stalk cutting" day. We had worked all summer to clear a tobacco field. Finally, every leaf was gone, leaving behind a field of naked stalks standing up defiantly. There is nothing quite like a teenager aiming the dual wheels of a Farmall tractor down the row and engaging the front-mounted stalk cutter. I always started slow, then slipped into a higher gear and pushed the throttle up. Before long I was soaring through the field, tobacco stalks flying all around.

After a summer of slow, tedious work, there was something about moving full speed through row after row, leaving nothing in my wake but an empty field. All the while grinning at the joy of cutting stalks. Often, I would have to stand to endure the bouncing, bucking Farmall, a special breed of tractor. Farmalls are small, light, unwieldy, but exceptionally flexible, which made them perfect for cutting stalks. I know now my joy came not just from the thrill of cutting stalks, but from the sense of completion. Over the summer my team and I had visited a single tobacco field six, seven, even eight times. Each week, I had pulled another group of ripe leaves or hung them in the barn until the very last leaf was gone. Looking back at an empty field seemed to reinforce a job well-done, closing the chapter on the summer until next spring's planting. I realize now the joy of that moment was, in fact, a reflection of doing the right thing well.

It is a wonderful thing to know the right thing to do. It is even better to stand firm and do the right thing. But what separates the saved and the unsaved, the believer and the unbeliever, is the ability to summon joy in any circumstance. Many secular leaders work hard. Many secular leaders discern the right thing to do with great skill. Many secular leaders even stand firm and administer the right thing with skill and perseverance. But few secular leaders consistently find and demonstrate joy, day in and day out.

Please don't think of joy as a regular, outward expression of giddiness. For a Christian, joy is finding an inward peace that reflects on those around you. Joy is not so much about how much you smile and laugh as about how content you are with everything about you. Certainly, smiling and laughing is a nice reflection of joy, but what sustains people is contentment, which exudes a level of happiness that others want to tap. My cousins and I fought for a chance to drive that Farmall through the field and cut stalks back in Farm Life. We shared the contentment that was the satisfaction of clearing those fields for the next year's planting.

As a leader, contentment brings people to your side. People want to follow those who find happiness in their circumstances. Conversely, no one wants to follow disgruntled, argumentative, and grumpy curmudgeons. As James tells us, Christians find joy in any circumstance because of our faith. Believers understand that those circumstances sharpen our capabilities to a finer point. Paul reminds us of this when he says he has found a way to be content in every circumstance.[40] I watch this contrast in my aging friends as one after another, their long-term careers evaporate when companies lay them off. Some are angry, and their daily countenance reflects this emotion. But many accept the disappointment and look beyond the unfortunate circumstances. Instead they seek new opportunities and options. Even as

---

[40] Philippians 4:11 *"Not that I am speaking of being in need, for I have learned in whatever situation I am to be content."*

those opportunities sometimes evade them, they remain content. Their joy comes not from their jobs, but from their God.

This doesn't mean Christians are never sad or disappointed. Christians live in the same world as everyone else. There is sadness in the world. We are a people under the curse of sin, and sadness is a normal output of that curse. Christians are certainly sad. Yet as Christians, even in the saddest times, we can call up our joy. I think of times when I have been at my lowest. Events like job failures, personal failures, disappointments. Yet the joy is still there, available for me. I may not always choose to grasp it, but when I am ready to move on, a reflection on a verse, or a well-placed song brings me around to the joy that comes not from myself, but from our Lord. That joy is there, ready and waiting for me.

I often felt low in Houston as we worked day after day on the pipeline project we all knew would lead to ruin. It can be difficult to serve on a sinking ship. My boss changed midstream, and the result was terrible. The new boss perhaps counts as my worst boss ever. He micromanaged, yelled, lost his temper, cursed, you name it. He also fired our contractor in the midst of the work, which added more delays and cost to the project. Only my faith and my family kept me together in that difficult time. I remember specifically thinking of James 1:2-4[41] late one cold night in Boston. God was lining me up for a full measure of joy in that time, as the trials stacked up one after another. Even though I was low, I knew God would teach me, and eventually deliver me from this project.

This is because a Christian's joy is not natural, but supernatural. Our joy comes directly from a great and sovereign God who by providence has given joy to His people. We have God's wellspring of joy. A never-ending fountain of grace covering the curse of sin with the redemption power of the blood of Jesus. The bumper sticker has it right, "Not Perfect, Just Forgiven."[42] God's family cannot help but find joy when covered by grace.

Joy begins with grace. Without grace there can be no sustaining joy. The grace of God frees us. This is what we celebrate. This is the source of our joy. Even in the worst circumstances there is faith that tomorrow will

---

[41] James 1:2-4 *"Count it all joy, my brothers, when you meet trials of various kinds, for you know that the testing of your faith produces steadfastness. And let steadfastness have its full effect, that you may be perfect and complete, lacking in nothing."*

[42] https://www.cafepress.com/+forgiven+bumper-stickers

be better. As Jesus told His disciples, *"So with you: Now is your time of grief, but I will see you again and you will rejoice, and no one will take away your joy."*[43] Now that is reason to celebrate. The time is coming when *no one* can take away your joy. If you want to demonstrate joy, you need to find a relationship with Jesus. Without Jesus your joy is but a fleeting moment, but with Jesus your joy is an everlasting fountain.

Joy also requires effective management of your *whole* life. You cannot isolate work and home and routinely find joy. Joy at work begins with joy at home as joy at home leads to joy at work. If you are not satisfied with your home life, you need to seek a solution. Perhaps the solution is prayer, counseling, or open discussion with your family. To reflect Christ at work, you must first become a reflection of Christ at home. If work is your refuge from a difficult home life, people notice. You cannot fake joy. Only once you have resolved to find joy at home can you hope to demonstrate joy when you work.

This is also true if home is your refuge from a difficult work life. You cannot consistently show joy if you cannot reconcile your circumstances at work. If you have a difficult boss, pray for him or her. If you have a difficult project, pray for guidance. If you have difficult employees, pray for them and deal with that relationship. If you face continued issues at work, find a way to bring joy to the situation. In the worst case, you may have to find a means to move on. You cannot hope to be a successful, motivated Christian leader in an impossible environment. If you cannot find a way to *"work heartily, as for the Lord,"*[44] find a way to work elsewhere.

Once you have a healthy relationship with God, a healthy relationship at home, and a healthy relationship with your job, you can embrace joy in all you do. Only then will people clearly see your joy. Only then will you be ready to demonstrate the third imperative of Christian leadership, "Find Joy in All You Do." The ten attributes that follow—purpose, passion, energy, respect, truth, trust, caring, courage, humility, and meekness—will provide a pathway for you.

However, finding joy always begins with prayer.

---

[43] John 16:22 NIV
[44] Colossians 3:23

Today, pause and pray that you might find joy in all circumstances.

Pray that the words on these pages serve as guides to the Spirit's direction for joy in your life. If you are in difficult circumstances at home or work, pray for insight and guidance. Pray that opportunities present themselves that you might demonstrate joy. Pray that you remember the things God may teach you as you face trials. Pray for your leaders, pray for your followers, pray for yourself, that you might fully align with God's plan for joy in all you do. Finally, thank God for your opportunities and praise Him for His leadership in your life.

DAY TWENTY
Imperative Three: Find Joy in All You Do

PURPOSE

"Purpose is the goal that someone wants to achieve, or that something is intended to achieve."[45]

Biblical Reference: Romans 8:28

"And we know that in all things God works for the good of those who love him, who have been called according to his purpose."

Nowhere is the joy of accomplishment more evident than in the construction business. I managed a great group of transmission construction crews at TVA. These men and women build large, tower-based power lines as a living. They spend most of their time on the road, living in campers, hotels, or pick-up trucks. They are a crusty bunch, hardened by constant life away from home, and by year-round outside work. They are also extraordinarily loyal and hard working. They find joy in their job, because more than any other occupation, they stand and see their accomplishments every day. But not every day is joyous. One of those difficult days occurred in the summer of 2013.

I got the call when I was at an annual customer meeting outside Nashville. A member of the public had died associated with an accident

---

[45] https://www.macmillandictionary.com/us/dictionary/american/purpose

on a construction job. Accidents can happen unexpectedly, and many times there is no one to blame. I needed to join my crew, but I could not travel for several hours. I had a commitment to speak to customers at that annual meeting, and I needed to stay for the speech. As soon as the meeting ended, I hit the road to the jobsite. All the way down I was thinking, how could I care for the crew? I knew they would be terribly upset, many of them traumatized by the gruesome event. In the car on the way down, I established a purpose, a short-term purpose for sure, but a purpose, nonetheless. My job was to represent my company well, and I did. But I also sought to demonstrate care and concern in this difficult time for this loyal group of hard-working people. I knew they were hurting, even if they didn't want anyone to see that.

When I arrived, I was shocked. Without sharing specifics, the scene of the accident was unpleasant and emotionally charged.

Because of my delay, one of my peers had arrived before me. He had already implemented his own purpose, which was considerably misaligned with mine. His purpose was above all else, to protect the company from lawsuits and damage. Perhaps he listened to the same people advising Tom Kilgore on the ash spill years earlier. This man treated the situation like a criminal investigation. He isolated each member of the crew. He even invited the local sheriff to join him as one by one they deposed and investigated each crew member. Our construction crew members felt like criminals.

I immediately stopped the process, thanked the sheriff, and told him I would let him know if I needed him again. Then I gathered all the men and women together in a conference room and apologized on behalf of my peer. I already knew enough to explain to them they were not to blame. The accident was the result of a failed piece of equipment. The crew had all safeguards in place but could not have anticipated this reliable component to have simply broken. This type of failure had never happened before in the history of TVA that we could determine. I dug deeper for their questions and concerns, and we went one by one around the room to hear how they were feeling about what they had experienced. Some of these hardened men and women shed tears as they shared their thoughts and concerns. At the end of the meeting I promised them TVA would stand with them. I gave them the number for our counseling service and told them to take the next day off, but stay together, don't go home, because I want you back in two days.

After the men and women left, I spent the evening with my peer who had fought for legal protection. We talked a long time about trading legal fortification for the feelings of loyal men and women. We talked about how those employees would never forget our actions on that day. How their opinions of our company would always come back to the treatment they received. He never agreed with me but conceded that this was my jurisdiction and that was that.

It was a terrible week. I spent time with the family of the deceased. I spent time with the media. I answered questions of our own safety people, of our own security people. I talked with our lawyers, with our communications team, with our human resources team. I talked to almost everyone that week. But the best time, the time I remember specifically about that week, is the time spent with my VP of construction, Clayton, and his crew. I visited them onsite a couple more times and each time we seemed to bond more deeply. I could see the improvement in them, and they could see that Clayton and I really cared for them. This was the bright spot in the week. Saturday afternoon, I attended the funeral and drove back home. I remember falling onto the couch and finally letting go, weeping for my crew, weeping for the loss in the family, and turning lose all the stress and anxiety of the week.

When I look back, I don't count that week as a week of joy. Yet the sustaining value of the week was accomplishing my purpose, which made all the pain worth enduring. Now when I look back, I look back with pride and joy for a job well done in a tough situation. I am sure all those men and women remember this experience in much the same way. This was clearly a strike on the anvil in the midst of a refiner's fire in each of our lives. I know it was a confirmation of the importance of faith for me.

As Christians we all have an overriding purpose in our lives. God made us to glorify Him in all we do.[46] His purpose guides us, strengthens us, helps us through difficult times. Having a purpose serves as a backdrop for evaluation. When facing a decision, we weigh our decision against our purpose. Does our decision glorify God—or not? Without a purpose,

---

[46] Isaiah 43:7 *"everyone who is called by my name, whom I created for my glory, whom I formed and made."*

decisions become random and confusing. Without a purpose, it is impossible to find joy in routine tasks. But when we center around a purpose, everything changes. When the tasks before us begin to add up to achieving a broader purpose, we find them easier to endure.

Think about something as simple as mowing your lawn. As you complete a section, you put that section behind you, and you move on to the next. Rather than look at how much remains, you take joy from the work already completed. Joy at work acts a bit like this. As you build toward your purpose, you can look back, see where you have been, and find joy in the journey toward your purpose.

Not every week will be joyous. That is why you need a purpose. Center yourself around the glorification of God. Then consider how you want to live your life. Make short and long-term goals. Define a direction for the near and the far. Keep your goals simple, keep them achievable, and keep them on track. A purpose has multiple, staged goals, just like mowing your lawn. First, I mow the left front, then the right front. Then I mow the side and finally the back. At each stage, I feel the joy of accomplishing a staged goal. My purpose is to mow the complete yard, yet sometimes, it just feels good to complete a section. Use goals as a boost of joy along the pathway to your purpose, particularly if your purpose is difficult, like rallying a team of construction workers after a catastrophic event. Even in tough times, a purpose serves as a means to joy. And joy in your life will automatically glorify God!

Ask yourself these questions:

- Do I recognize my long-term purpose to glorify God?
- Do I set staged goals and establish a purpose in my life?
- Do I regularly test my purpose against my Christian values?

Today, pray for purpose in your leadership.

Pray that the Holy Spirit will open your mind to the purpose that serves the moment well. Pray Romans 8:28 that you will align with God's purpose for your life and that all that occurs will eventually work for good. Confess your shortfalls and pray for improvement. Pray for moral purpose in your leaders, pray for your followers to recognize the actions of your purpose. Pray God will present you with an opportunity to confirm and live out your purpose. Pray that God will strengthen your faith so you might lean on Him in your life, both at work and at home. Finally, thank God for your opportunities and praise Him for His leadership in your life.

DAY TWENTY-ONE
Imperative Three: Find Joy in All You Do

PASSION

"Passion is an intense, driving, or overmastering feeling or conviction."[47]

Biblical Reference: Colossians 3:23-24

"Whatever you do, work heartily, as for the Lord and not for men, knowing that from the Lord you will receive the inheritance as your reward. You are serving the Lord Christ."

There are so many examples of passion around us. My favorite passionate leader is my friend, Buddy Rogers. Buddy leads thousands of transmission workers now at Duke Energy. His legendary passion marks his entire career. Anytime there is an emergency Buddy is the first volunteer. He led 250 people to Louisiana after Katrina, sleeping in tents and helping to restore power. He led the same size group to Florida after Hurricane Charley. He has led innumerable teams and restored electricity to millions of homes. When Buddy steps up, people sign on. People seek out his team. Everyone wants to go with Buddy. He cares for his people. He is no-nonsense focused and highly capable. But above all his passion never

---

[47] https://www.merriam-webster.com/dictionary/passion

fades, even after long days sleeping in tents, armories, or gymnasiums. Buddy's passion is an integral part of his Christian leadership. His passion reinforces his witness and demonstrates how living for Christ brings joy in all circumstances.

The apostle Paul says, *"Whatever you do, work heartily, as for the Lord."* Why would Paul write so forcefully about work? He specifically frames the issue with "Whatever you do," meaning in *everything* you do. We are to work heartily, as for the Lord and not for men or women. How much more intense would you work if you were serving Jesus? With Jesus as our client, work would be true joy. We would be serving the Lord directly. This is exactly why we do all work as if we are working for the Lord. Paul understood this as he wrote these words with the guiding of the Holy Spirit. When we think of work as for the Lord, we can find joy there. Paul tells us to work heartily, an interesting word that has multiple meanings. The Greek word Paul uses means "from the soul." In everything we do, we should work from the soul as for the Lord.

Consider Galatians 5:22-23 as Paul lists the gifts of the Spirit.[48] There he references *"the one who leads, with zeal."* Leadership is a gift of the Spirit, and Paul guides us by defining how we are to lead, with *zeal!* We use the word *passion* more often than zeal, but they are largely interchangeable. The Bible is clear. We should lead with passion, which is God's way of bringing joy to tough situations.

For a moment think of the original audience of the book of Colossians. Many of these people led difficult lives with terrible jobs. A number were likely slaves in this Roman province. Yet Paul instructs them to work heartily as for the Lord. By doing so, they gained a certain power over their masters. They became happy even in tough conditions, because they were able to look beyond their current plight. This is one way God brings joy to our lives, even as we work in difficult circumstances. As a Christian leader how could you fail to be obedient in this fundamental request? Bring passion to your work and you will find joy.

But you must also bring passion so others might follow. Like Buddy Rogers, for example. Buddy shows his people that he cares for them openly and often. He attends the funerals of their loved ones, he visits them in

---

[48] Galatians 5:22-23 *"But the fruit of the Spirit is love, joy, peace, forbearance, kindness, goodness, faithfulness, gentleness and self-control. Against such things there is no law."*

the hospital, he prays with them, he walks beside them in difficult times. People *know* they can always count on Buddy, not because Buddy has made passion a priority in his life, but because passion is an integral part of him. His passion flows, even when it's not the perfect moment to express passion. Buddy's wife describes making Buddy sit on the visitor's side during their son's wrestling matches, because his passion flows so freely during the match and embarrasses the home team. People who follow Buddy understand his passion is always there, and they line up to follow him because his passion spreads to them as followers.

Passion is a key requirement of great leadership. Passion is infectious. Passion spreads to followers like cat videos on social media. When you lead with passion, your team works with passion. In that way, they find their joy, even if they are not believers in the Word. Think of this as a part of your mission. You show passion and find joy in your work. By doing so, you transmit passion to all those you lead and give them a pathway to joy as well. This passion transfer becomes a part of your Christian leadership, and as such becomes a testimony for all to see.

So how do you find passion? This is easy if you are working on something you love and enjoy. But this can be very difficult if you don't feel passionate. If this is you, consider how you might find your passion, or perhaps regain it. Maybe a vacation, or another job assignment, or a new project. Maybe you need to pray unceasingly that God gifts you with passion. The very best way to find passion is to do work you enjoy. I loved working in the energy business. Every few months, we successfully fought a natural disaster that demanded a passionate response. As teams and people came together to restore power, we commanded a central goal and purpose. The results were easy to track. And best of all, the hubris of day-to-day mediocrity found its way to the back burner. The focus was on one thing only. Everyone rallied around that one important goal.

If you are struggling to find joy in your work, look to see if you have lost your passion, which ebbs naturally without regular stimulation and renewal. You need to pay attention to your passion and nurture it. Work to keep passion by shifting projects, balancing workload, and seeking new opportunities. Renew your passion regularly. Just as every time you open the Word of God, every time you pray, every time you praise and worship God, you are renewing the passion within your soul for Jesus Christ.

Ask yourself these questions:

- Do I feel passion for the work I do?
- Do I work to keep my passion for work refreshed?
- Do I ask God to give me passion for my work so that I might work heartily?

Today, pray for a passion for your work.

Pray that the Holy Spirit fills you with a passion for what you do. Pray Colossians 3:23-24 that you work heartily and internalize the idea that you are "working as for the Lord." Confess your shortfalls and pray for improvement. Pray for passion in your leaders, pray for infectious passion in your followers. Pray God will present you with an opportunity to demonstrate passion. Pray that God will strengthen your faith that you might learn to work as for Him. Finally, thank God for your opportunities and praise Him for His leadership in your life.

DAY TWENTY-TWO
Imperative Three: Find Joy in All You Do

ENERGY

> "Energy is the exertion of power; the capacity to do work."[49]

Biblical Reference: Isaiah 4:28-31

> "Have you not known? Have you not heard? The Lord is the everlasting God, the Creator of the ends of the earth. He does not faint or grow weary; his understanding is unsearchable. He gives power to the faint, and to him who has no might he increases strength. Even youths shall faint and be weary, and young men shall fall exhausted; but they who wait for the Lord shall renew their strength; they shall mount up with wings like eagles; they shall run and not be weary; they shall walk and not faint."

Years ago, I sang in a gospel quartet. We had a wonderful time and traveled quite a bit, sharing God's love through our enjoyment as we sang. Churches loved to turn their Sunday night service over to us, and we really enjoyed having that kind of freedom and time to sing all we wanted. But

---

[49] https://medical-dictionary.thefreedictionary.com/Energy+(biology)

there was one big problem. They always fed us. Anyone who has been an invited guest of a church understands the challenge. There would be casseroles, lots of meat, mashed potatoes, and dessert after dessert. The buffet was always delicious, and always destroyed my ability to hit the high notes.

I sang tenor, and we had several songs that were really up there. I learned from experience not to overeat, because the notes just would not appear when the time came. Night after night, I would eat like a bird while all the church members would try their best to stuff me full. The rest of the guys thought this was funny, although our baritone and lead also had to hold back a little. This was *not true* of our bass singer. The more he ate, the lower he seemed to sing.

Except one night.

This beautiful church had fed us as usual with a huge spread, and Mr. Bass had tried every dish. He had piled the meats, potatoes, casseroles, and deserts on, plate after plate. When it came time to start the service, we decided to begin with an a cappella song. On this song, our bass sang an entry line, and we all took our notes from his line. I hit his pitch on the piano, and he was supposed to begin. Mr. Bass did, but he was nowhere near the piano pitch. He was painfully off.

He stopped.

I hit his note again.

He tried a second time.

Once again, a different painful note.

He stopped.

By this time, the whole church was looking around. I suspect trying to determine if these guys were worth their home-cooked meal. Finally, Mr. Bass looked at the crowd and said, "Folks, if you are going to feed me that much, you can't expect me to be able to sing too." We skipped the acapella song and moved to the next one. He fell in just fine from that point forward, but never ate that much before singing again.

The lesson? Think about your energy and plan your intake around your desired outtake. Sometimes this doesn't work. Presenting yourself well after a fourteen-hour, red-eye flight from Korea requires an extra reserve of energy. I once went to a job interview the very next day after returning from Korea. *That went well*, I thought. *I tried very hard to be upbeat and energetic* (hard enough at 7 A.M.). I must have been okay; I got the job. However, some months later one of the interviewers told me, "I thought you were pretty tired." Find a way to draw deep on your energy reserve and learn how to turn that reserve on and off when you need to. Even if someone tells you later you looked tired.

Everyone has energy within them. For some energy flows constantly. These people are always up, always alive with excitement. These people remind us of puppies going full speed until they drop, then they sleep and wake again at full speed. Not everyone can sustain puppy-like energies. Many people like to operate at slower speeds, more of the middle-aged cat lying in wait until the moment is necessary, then striking with power and poise. Leaders have an internal energy source just like everyone else. But unlike everyone else, leaders must know how to dig the energy well deeper on demand.

Energy is a prerequisite for true leadership, and essential for joy. Not all interactions require high energy, but when they do, high energy may be essential to success. Consider your own experience with leadership. Do you follow the leader who presents with passion and energy, or the one who appears to be sleepwalking through his or her message?

Controlling your own energy is challenging. Perhaps it is easy enough to ramp up the caffeine in the morning and hold your energy level through the next cup. But what about 2 P.M. after a big lunch? Have you sat through after-lunch meetings and left with a poor impression of the speaker? Or perhaps you don't recall what the speaker said? Controlling your energy requires forethought and action. If you face a big meeting in the morning, you may need to get up earlier than usual. For many people a good workout helps to get energy levels up. For others you may need a light breakfast, or a big cup of coffee. Know how you build your energy and use your knowledge to set yourself up for success. This is particularly true after lunch, which is well known as the toughest time to grab attention. This is not just true for those listening, but also for the leader.

An after-lunch leader needs to be more energetic than at any other time. This is the time when others need to draw upon your energy. There is one big way to influence your own energy and that is to control your intake. The greatest contribution to post-lunch naps is carbohydrates. A heavy carb meal will draw your energy down, and you will find yourself fighting to stay alert. If you have a big meeting or presentation after lunch, eat light, eat healthy, or don't eat at all.

Energy is an essential part of finding your joy. If you are tired, your joy may be taking a break. If you are bored, your joy may be side-lined. If you are distracted, your joy may be idling. You need energy to enjoy what you are doing. If you find yourself constantly low on energy, examine your life. Are you working too many hours? Do you have too many activities? Or maybe you just have young kids and your sleep is poor. Everyone has days of low energy and followers even allow leaders to have low energy from time to time.

But consistent, constant low energy is the same as posting a sign on your forehead saying, "Find a leader elsewhere." You might manage people, but you will never lead them. Perhaps the only exception is when your people know you have a young child and then they give you some leeway. Even then, when something really important comes up, find a way to get the sleep you need.

When I am tired, I try to think of Isaiah 4:28-31, which is a key verse for this entire book. How can you read these words and not find inspiration? As a Christian, think about running without being weary. Think about soaring on wings of eagles. Think about walking or doing a project for a long time without feeling tired (faint). Think about the Lord's promise to renew your energy. Before you step into an important moment, think of these words and pray for renewed strength. Pray for the Holy Spirit to take over. Pump yourself up with the words of the Bible. They are always there, even when your energy level may not be. You can rely on the Lord. You can call on the Lord. You can draw from the infinite energy that is the Lord's and apply that energy in your situation. If you are truly a leader, you know when you need energy. Eat well, rest well, and pray yourself up.

Ask yourself these questions:

- Do I consciously reflect energy when I lead?
- Do I plan to ensure I will be at my best when the time comes?
- Do I pray for help and draw energy from God when I have exhausted my reserve?

Today, pray for energy.

Pray that the Holy Spirit upholds you with energy when the time is right. Pray Isaiah 4:28-31 to renew your strength and inspire your soul by the power and wisdom of our Lord. Confess your shortfalls and pray for improvement. Pray for energy in your leaders, pray for your followers to see your energy and reflect your energy back with their own energy. Pray God will present you with an opportunity to demonstrate energy to others. Pray that God will strengthen your faith that He might augment your good habits with a deep well of energy when you need it. Finally, thank God for your opportunities and praise Him for His leadership in your life.

DAY TWENTY-THREE
Imperative Three: Find Joy in All You Do.

RESPECT

"Respect is a high or special regard."[50]

Biblical Reference: 1 Peter 2:17 (NIV)

"Show proper respect to everyone, love the family of believers, fear God, honor the emperor."

Mrs. Rudisill was angry. Every time a thunderstorm rolled through, her power went off. Every time. The linemen had yet to solve the problem, so why not give the new guy a try? Fresh from North Carolina State, this new engineer should have an answer. This is how "Tater" and I ended up out in the country that day. "Tater" isn't his real name, of course. It's his lineman name. Linemen have names like Snake, Rabbit, Bud. Never their real names.

On this day, Tater and I were at Mrs. Rudisill's house. She had the unfortunate luck of being at the end of a very long, 25,000-volt distribution line. That's 25 kV, although since she was on a single-phase line, any good engineer divides 25kV by the square root of three and knows her actual voltage is closer to 13,900 volts. Still more than 100 times what comes from your outlet, and enough to power the county. And perfect for Mrs.

---

[50] https://www.merriam-webster.com/dictionary/respect

Rudisill's transformer in her front yard. None of this mattered to Mrs. Rudisill. She only cared that her lights were out.

Tater and I were alone that day in a pickup truck with no tools. Lucky for us, Tater grabbed his rubber gloves—25,000-volt gloves, by the way. Mrs. Rudisill lived on an underground tap line, a single-phase transformer at the end of a radial underground line. Underground transformers are the green boxes sitting on top of the ground. Inside them insulated cables end with 90-degree elbow joints connecting to a transformer bushing. Think of a transformer bushing as the receptacle the elbow joints plug into, just like the receptacles on your wall, only a lot bigger. The only exposed energized parts are where the elbows and the bushings connect. We opened her transformer but could see nothing wrong.

Then Tater had an idea. How many unfortunate outcomes begin with "Tater had an idea"? We didn't have a hot stick with us, the device used to pull energized elbows out of the transformer, so Tater improvised, donned his rubber gloves, and pulled the elbow out with his hands. This is very much against the safety rules because this means Tater is holding in his hands a "hot" elbow, with the exposed tip energized to 13,900 volts. He looked around inside the transformer for a few minutes but complained that he couldn't see anything while still holding that stiff elbow in his gloved hand. Every time he tried to bend down and look, the elbow was in his way. With the tip of that elbow energized at 13,900 volts, he had to be very careful where he held it. We worked out a solution. He placed the elbow in his left hand and shook off his right glove. Then I took his right glove and the hot elbow.

Now Tater could wiggle around, spotting a pinhole under the transformer bushing, only a couple feet above the ground. A pinhole in the bushing meant lightning had bored a small exit hole through the insulation and was shorting out against the side of the green transformer cabinet. Every time lightning was in the area, Mrs. Rudisill's transformer was the most attractive route to ground. And every time there was a storm, there was a short in her transformer, which blew the fuse in her line. She was out of power, over and over again. Seeing the hole, Tater said something simple, like "Look at that!!"

I looked. When someone called Tater says do something, you do it. That's when time slowed to a crawl. As I leaned over, the tip of the energized elbow came down with me and inadvertently touched one of Mrs. Rudisill's beautiful rose bushes. At that point, all those stored-up electrons found an immediate, attractive pathway to ground. When electrons travel rapidly to ground like that, you get a nice blue fire and a loud thrumming noise.

I turned to the fire and immediately thought, *That's what a 25,000-volt fault looks like six inches from my hand.* Of course, being an engineer, my next thought was, *It's not 25,000 volts, you have to divide by the square root of three, so it's really only 13,900 volts.* And that's also when I thought about Moses. Is this what the burning bush looked like? I wondered. About that time physics took over and the bush disappeared.

Not just burned up, gone.

Evaporated.

Invisible.

Not like Moses at all.

It was deathly quiet. In the distance Tater and I could hear the *squeak, squeak* sound of yet another blown fuse at Mrs. Rudisill's house. Fuses are mounted at the top of poles inside a swinging barrel that swings up and locks in when energized, but falls out, swinging away when the fuse blows. This allows a troubleshooter to drive down the road and spot blown fuses from the ground. It also means the barrel will swing back and forth after blowing, making a squeaking sound you really would not want to hear when you are working on an energized line. The squeak of the fuse barrel means you messed up. You somehow contacted an energized line. That squeak also means a lot of paperwork, a power outage, a lost rosebush (we never mentioned that to Mrs. Rudisill), and potentially someone getting hurt. That's the *squeak, squeak* we heard. This is when Tater uttered the predictable expletive.

Electricity demands respect. This 25,000-volt, distribution-line problem was my first brush with the power of high voltage electrons in motion. About a year later, I sat in the gravel parking lot of a substation, thanking God for provision, having just come within inches of killing myself. I was looking for a transformer bushing fault on a substation transformer. Substation transformers are huge, this one was the size of a recreational vehicle. On top are the bushings where the high voltage enters the transformer. These bushings are just like those in Mrs. Rudisill's transformer, only much, much bigger. Occasionally, the insulators on those bushings will crack or break and create a problem. This is what I was looking for that day.

I grabbed the top edge of the six-foot tall transformer and pulled myself up, high enough to see the bushing, a bit like jumping up to the bottom tier pole in the tobacco barn. Unfortunately, this put my head within inches of the minimum approach distance. The minimum approach distance is vitally important when working with extremely high voltage, like the 110,000 volts on top of this particular transformer bushing. Minimum approach means: Do not approach inside this minimum distance. For 110,000 volts, that is about four feet or so. The bushing itself is about three feet tall, so by lifting my head above the transformer top, which was the same level as the bushing, my head was approaching *three* feet from 110,000 volts.

Inside the minimum approach distance, electrons react and jump through the air. Once a grounded object (like someone with their hand on a transformer) enters this distance, electrons will arc over and select that pathway to ground. Everyone has seen demonstrations of electricity arcing colorfully through the air. That is exactly what happens. No one wants to be on the other side of a 110,000 electrical arc. Electricity at that voltage level enters the body and cooks you from the inside out. Contact with high-voltage electricity destroys organs and leads to almost certain death. As I sat in my car that day, I wondered if I could ever trust myself in a substation again. I had lost my *respect* for electricity. I had lost my concentration and I did something dumb and dangerous.

Soon titles like Supervisor, Superintendent, Manager, VP followed. With these titles came responsibility, part of which was dealing with bad things. Over the years I saw many results of electricity out of control. I attended funerals and settled claims, and my respect for electricity continued to grow. Everyone knows electricity can be dangerous, but only with experience after experience does respect blossom. Each new experience with high voltage built another layer on my foundational respect for electricity. This is not unique. From this layered respect for electricity, people have learned to put electrons to work, lighting up the Piedmont Carolinas, the Tennessee Valley, the whole world.

Respect for leaders works a lot like respect for electricity. You may have a title of leader, but you don't gain respect until your people actually have hands-on experience of your leadership. Similar to how I learned to experience the power of electricity from many hands-on experiences with that tremendous power. People learn to respect you as a leader when they experience over and over again your good leadership skills. As a leader, situations and circumstances demonstrate if you are worthy of the respect of others. If you repeatedly know and do the right thing, respect grows for you from your people. You earn respect experience by experience.

Think of respect as a series of layers, like my experience with electricity. You begin with a little, but how you act either erodes or builds another layer upon your foundation. Compare this to icing a cake. First the bottom layer, interesting, but not yet a cake. Each layer you add, the better the cake becomes, at least until you build a complete cake. This is how layers of respect work. You start with the bottom layer of a relationship. Each experience adds another layer of respect until you have built a complete picture where others respect you.

But respect is a two-way street. Any respect you earn is quickly dashed if you fail to demonstrate respect for the people you lead. Once again, the Bible teaches us about respect. Peter teaches in 1 Peter 2:17 to respect others—*everyone*, in fact. When we respect others, we demonstrate the very behavior we seek in return. Peter tells us to love our fellow believers, to be engaged and actively involved with others who believe. This is a call to church participation. Active church engagement adds layers of respect from your church family. As people see you leading in Bible-based activities, people see you as a Christian leader. People layer in another level of icing on the respect cake. I can't tell you how many times through the years I have found employees who were successful at their jobs and were also leaders in their churches. Church leadership earns respect and builds confidence that leaks over from the church to permeate how people perform at work. Think of your church activity as a safe place to explore and practice how you build your layers of respect at work.

Peter tells us to fear God, meaning to respect God. The fear or respect of God keeps us in our place, understanding our role in the bigger picture of life. The fear of God directs our lives and shapes our outward countenance. This respect for God is evident in our lives. Respect flows in and out of our lives. We give it and we seek it in return. Respect is essential as a leader. We need it to be successful, and we must give it to earn it. As we demonstrate respect for God, and we demonstrate respect for the people we lead, and we demonstrate leadership skills and decisions worthy of respect, only then do we earn the respect that is necessary for effective leadership.

Finally, Peter tells us we must also respect the emperor. In other words, we respect authority. If we desire respect, we need to respect our own authority. People watch, they learn from us. If we respect our boss, our company, our government, then they tend to respect us in the same way.

You want respect, give it. Then wait for the layers to grow. Respect is essential if you wish to enjoy what you do each day. Respect is critical if you wish to lead. Respect is eternal when you lead with the fear of God in your soul.

Ask yourself these questions:

- Do I respect others first, like my followers, my boss?
- Am I actively engaged in loving other believers?
- Do I have a relationship with God that demonstrates respect throughout my life?

Today, pray for respect.

Pray that the Holy Spirit will guide you to respect others, to fear God, and to respect authority. Pray 1 Peter 2:17 that your actions might demonstrate respect. Confess your shortfalls and pray for improvement. Pray for respect in your leaders, pray for your followers to recognize your countenance and help you to add layers of respect for your own leadership, based on good actions. Pray God will present you with an opportunity to demonstrate an added layer of respect. Pray that God will strengthen your faith that you might grow in respect for Him. Finally, thank God for your opportunities and praise Him for His leadership in your life.

DAY TWENTY-FOUR
Imperative Three: Find Joy in All You Do

TRUTH

"Truth is the property of being in accord with fact or reality."[51]

Biblical Reference: Colossians 3:9

"Do not lie to one another, seeing that you have put off the old self with its practices."

Soon after joining TVA, I sought to find a way my employees might know more about me. I developed an idea of writing an online "Blog" from the Executive Vice President. The idea was to share current issues and ideas with anyone who had access to our internal system. Built into the blog was a question-and-answer forum. I intended to write about current issues, then address a question or two.

But things did not turn out that way. After the very first writing, I received dozens of questions. All the questions were difficult, probing, and challenging. I answered each one and found a great gap in knowledge between management and employees. Because employees could ask pretty much anything anonymously, submitting questions online became a popular way to ask exactly what was on their minds. I tried to answer

---

[51] https://www.macmillandictionary.com/us/dictionary/american/truth

each question openly and clearly, but I found it was challenging to do so and stay within policy and procedures. I would pull in HR and Legal and have long discussions before posting an answer. Often the answer would make management representatives uncomfortable. Within a few days, the blog was no more, but the question-and-answer forum stayed open, and the questions kept coming.

I tried to share as much information as I knew. I found that employees welcomed my being open and transparent, but I did not see the same response from management. At the time I had about 600 employees with online access. There were weeks the Q & A was tracking thousands of hits, because employees from all over TVA were reading my answers, not just my 600 employees. Plain answers were in great demand.

Soon my answers led to an invitation from the local union hall. The International Brotherhood of Electrical Workers (IBEW) represented TVA line workers as well as the Duke Energy line workers. They asked if I would meet them at the hall in Nashville and talk about several concerning issues. TVA's Director of Union Affairs insisted he join me, and we traveled to meet with about fifty union stewards from across the Tennessee Valley. We listened mostly, although from time to time I would answer their questions. Many times, my response was not the answer the stewards wanted to hear. Often, I just said, no we cannot do that. However, anytime I shared a no, I tried to explain why my response was no. The union stewards usually disagreed, but they appreciated my insight.

I took more than fifty action items from the meeting and eventually dealt with all of them. At least half were rejecting their requests but sharing the truth. These stewards loved it. They had never had such a frank conversation with management. All previous conversations had been careful and conservative with the objective to walk away with as few action items as possible. Turns out we had been doing a great job managing our union workers but a terrible job leading them.

Speaking the truth should be simple. Most people tell the truth, at least most of the time. Yet leadership and truthfulness seem to compete at times. Often this comes from company policy or procedure. A carefully thought-out plan or set of rules determines both the timing and specific information for sharing. It is unusual to find leaders who overtly lie to their people, though this happens. However, it is not all that unusual to find leaders who share partial truths with people, or maybe shades of truth. Leaders shy away from sharing too much, just in case people aren't ready for the full truth.

Most leaders have accepted the partial truth approach in some fashion. Our communications training specifically guides us to layer truth in components that might be more acceptable. We should guide people to the truth with care and ease. In other words, we spin it.

It's not a layoff, it is a "right-sizing."

It's not a shutdown, it's a "temporary pause in operations."

It's not losing money, it's a "temporary reduction of revenue."

We condition ourselves to think if the message doesn't sound too bad, then the reality of the circumstances must not be as bad. Our employees find this to be ridiculous. They are frustrated by their inability to get real answers about their futures. They look to their leaders for answers and instead get messages crafted to say as little as possible.

Shading the truth is epidemic among corporations. Leaders should push back, find a way to go beyond the current practice. When you go the extra mile, you will demonstrate to your employees that they are valuable enough to understand the circumstances that lie ahead. They see this as leadership. Not everyone will agree. Look at Jesus, many times even His disciples didn't agree with His blunt style. Your management will likely feel threatened if you push the truth envelope. Rather than bully your way through, finesse your way through. Find allies. Find policy loopholes. Share your plans. Be as open with your own management as you are with your employees.

As a Christian leader, look to Jesus for how to share the truth. When Jesus shares living water with the Samaritan woman at the well, He calls her out with a direct truth. *"You are right when you say you have no husband. The fact is, you have had five husbands, and the man you now have is not your husband. What you have just said is quite true."*[52] Jesus does not shade the truth. He does not divide the truth into comfortable increments. Consider Jesus as the Pharisees seek a sign and instead, He says, *"An evil and adulterous generation craves for a sign."*[53] He goes on to pronounce *"woes"* on the Pharisees in Mathew 23. Yet as Jesus faces the Pharisees on

---

[52] John 4:17-18 (NIV)
[53] Matthew 12:38 (NIV)

trial, He truthfully acknowledges that He is the Son of God, knowing this will lead to His death. Jesus never turns away from the full truth.

The result of being truthful is joy. After all, *"the truth will set you free."*[54] How much more joy can you find in your work if you are sharing the truth? Certainly, the converse is also true. How difficult is it to be joyous when you are hiding the truth or sharing lies or shades of truth?

Love the truth. Share the truth. And enjoy the results.

Ask yourself these questions:

- Do I regularly share the truth, or am I comfortable sharing partial truth or shades of truth?
- Do I understand policies and procedures well enough to know how to finesse the rules so I can speak truth?
- Can I say no when no is the right answer (and explain why)?

Today, pray for truth in your work life.

Pray that the Holy Spirit guides you to truth and reminds you if you stray away. Pray Colossians 3:9—"Do not lie to one another"—and put on your new self so you recognize untruth. Confess your shortfalls and pray for improvement. Pray for your leaders to speak truth, pray for your followers to recognize truth and accept it even when that truth is in opposition to their expectations. Pray God will present you with an opportunity to demonstrate sharing truth. Pray that God will strengthen your faith so you might grow in confidence for sharing truth. Finally, thank God for your opportunities and praise Him for His leadership in your life.

---

[54] John 8:32 (NIV)

DAY TWENTY-FIVE
Imperative Three: Find Joy in All You Do

TRUST

"Trust is the assured reliance on the character, ability, strength, or truth of someone or something."[55]

Biblical Reference: Proverbs 28:26

"Those who trust in themselves are fools, but those who walk in wisdom are kept safe."

I stumbled into a trust relationship. The Duke Carolinas team was a mess. Our recent layoff (right sizing?) left us shorthanded, short-skilled, and short of direction. Somehow, I emerged from the jumble with the assignment of VP of Field Operations, Carolinas, for Duke Energy. The people who were working to keep the lights on for North and South Carolina were all working for me it seemed. This proud group of people had been accustomed to seven complex layers of rule-based management. The new structure only left three layers. There was me, my leaders, and the first-line supervisors for a couple thousand folks. Only eight of us to manage line workers, engineers, and contractors for all of North and South Carolina.

We held our first meeting offsite to figure out how things would work.

---

[55] https://www.merriam-webster.com/dictionary/trust

I remember thinking about the process and concluding there was no way I could serve as a traditional boss. I could never hope to be involved in every decision. I could never sign off or validate each choice. There were too many choices to be made and we were just too flat as an organization. I would spend all my time bogged down in administrative affairs unless I gave up power, pushing authority down to my team. Like all good leaders in the 1990s, I put together a PowerPoint presentation. I think I had only one slide, which simply said, "It's Just Us." A long discussion followed. I remember stressing that we were all there was. This was no great leadership insight; this was just the way things were. Anything good that happened, we could claim those results. Anything bad that happened, we had to also claim those results. This incredibly talented group of leaders decided to trust each other, to trust me, to trust our experience and our instincts, and to just try to do what was right.

We eliminated rules-based approvals. I raised the leader financial approvals to unprecedented levels, and we trusted each other. Leaders ran their teams the best they knew how. When they needed help, I was there for them, but they hardly ever needed help. They loved it. I loved it. This was the freest any of us had ever been and that freedom was truly joyous. This freedom grew from desperation, but the foundation of our freedom was trust.

Of course, trust cannot be blind. Trust is an acquired skill that grows from prior experience with the basics of the work and also with the workers. The Duke Carolinas leaders had worked together for years. As a leader, your responsibility is to trust the right people at the right times. I worked several years at another organization where the mandate said to trust everyone in the company. However, the rules did not reflect this mandate. Here leaders were micro-managed with a tight rein on financial approvals. No decisions moved forward without several people's signoffs. No one in this company was willing to trust anyone else to make decisions that directly impacted themselves. It was a great company, but the lack of trust stood as a barrier for finding joy at work. Leaders cannot allow this. Leaders must know when and how to delegate responsibility and learn to live within their own delegations.

Likewise, leaders should know when *not* to trust. Some people, processes, and structures do not warrant trust. This may require an in-depth understanding. Before you reject trust, invest in the background work to truly understand situations. Dig just as deeply to understand where you must withdraw trust as you would when awarding your trust. That means you understand how the organization runs and how individuals complement or inhibit the process. Trusting those who bring poor results is a poor reflection on you as a leader. However, as a Christian, you have added insight.

We begin new life by trusting in Jesus. As a Christian, we are placing our eternal life in the hands of Christ. As the Perfect Savior, there is no better place to trust our future. The Bible tells us that Jesus took our place on the cross. He accepted the outcomes of our lives, particularly our sin. We understand what it means to place our trust in someone else, Jesus. We understand the ramifications of failing in that trust, of violating that trust. We have experienced the give-and-take of failure and repentance. This experience is exactly the experience we count upon to leverage trust in those with whom we work. When we trust a worker, we are willing to accept the outcome of his or her work as our own. After all, Jesus trusted the disciples to spread the word across Judea, Samaria, and even to the ends of the earth. Jesus gives us a deeper understanding of consequences and relationships. Jesus gives Christian leaders an extra measure of discernment when it comes to trust.

We have a perfect example.

Ask yourself these questions:

- Do I trust others, even when I know my reputation may depend on the outcome?
- Am I able to discern who is worthy of trust from those who require tighter management?
- Do I actively delegate and leverage trust, using the example set by Jesus?

Today, pray for good use of trust in your life and work.

Pray that the Holy Spirit will not only give you discernment, but also the desire to properly apply trust. Pray Proverbs 28:26 that you will walk in wisdom and learn to accept the wisdom and work ethics of others in your life. Confess your shortfalls and pray for improvement. Pray for trust in your leaders, pray for your followers to return your trust positively. Pray God will present you with an opportunity to demonstrate a new understanding of trust in your relationships. Pray that God will strengthen your own trust in Him so that you might apply this trust to others and find true joy in your work. Finally, thank God for your opportunities and praise Him for His leadership in your life.

DAY TWENTY-SIX
Imperative Three: Find Joy in All You Do.

CARING

> "*Caring is feeling or showing concern for, or kindness to others.*"[56]

Biblical Reference: Colossians 3:12

> "*Therefore, as God's chosen people, holy and dearly loved, clothe yourselves with compassion, kindness, humility, gentleness and patience.*"

Tom Smitherman was in trouble. As the COO for Nantahala Power Company, he was responsible for reliable electricity across his company. On this day in the late 1990s, Tom was not successful. The past two days had seen record amounts of snowfall. Not the fluffy, playful kind of snow, but the brutal, windy, wet, sticky snow that piled up in small mountains and stuck to everything. Enough snow had stuck to trees and power lines that Tom was facing unprecedented damage. He only had one choice, call for help.

Tom was fortunate that Duke Power Company had just bought his company. Duke had plenty of resources and a newfound obligation to help. I got the call on Sunday afternoon, about 3 P.M. Duke Power tapped four

---

[56] https://www.merriam-webster.com/dictionary/caring

of us to travel up to Nantahala and assess the situation. We were to be the front people for the recovery support effort. By the time we gathered, drove the four-hour trip, and found Tom, it was almost midnight. We met him in his office where he began to pump us up. "I handpicked each of you specifically." (Tom was an ex-Duke employee). "I need your individual skill sets to pull off this impossible task. I know you can each be successful, and I need you."

Tom gave a great speech. We could feel the compassion he felt for his customers and the trust he placed in us. The four of us split the area into quarters and charged into action. Three days later I was scrambling for line resources when a long convoy of line trucks drove by. I chased them down and found their leader. I told him I wanted to abscond his trucks and put them to work immediately. Their leader challenged me. "Hold on a minute," he said. "Tom told me he handpicked me for an impossible mission. I am not sure I can be diverted."

Turns out Tom handpicked any and every one willing to step into his office. What looked like compassion was instead desperation. We all laughed about Tom's tactics, marveled at his ingenuity and ability to motivate. But we were no longer so sure about being handpicked for an impossible mission.

I can empathize with Tom. I have always cared deeply for the people I lead, but have not always communicated that caring effectively. One year at TVA, I received a beautifully wrapped Christmas gift from one of my staff. I tore into the package and found the book *1001 Ways to Recognize Your Employees*. Okay, that is a questionable gift. I felt there must be a motivation here other than making me happy with a Christmas gift. Nonetheless, I shrugged it off and tossed the book in the pile with the rest of the obligatory self-help and leadership books. *I might get to it one day*, I thought.

Only a couple days later, I got another gift from a different staff member. Again, I tore into the package, anxious to see inside. *1001 Ways to Recognize Your Employees* was beneath the ribbons and bow. I got the message. I realized that I had earned these gifts. I believed that payday was sufficient recognition, and anything else was superfluous. So I read the book and learned a lot about showing how you care. I only read one of them though.

It is immensely difficult to find joy in anything you care nothing about, but caring is fundamental to joy. Who finds joy in watching sports after your team falters? Only those who care for the sport itself can watch teams play once their favorite team is out. This same fundamental is true for leading people. You cannot lead with joy unless you care for the people you lead. There are plenty of leaders who lead without caring, but none with sustaining joy. Perhaps there is joy in objectives achieved, goals conquered, or promotions gained. But all these are short-term joys. The joy of achievement fades as memory fades. The joy of goals conquered disappears with the next challenge. And the joy of promotion diminishes as the reality of the new responsibility begins to settle in. To find sustaining joy, you need to seek a source of joy that sticks with you over time.

What is the most consistent aspect of a leader's life? People. By definition, if you are leading, someone other than you will be involved. You are leading people. Perhaps the names and faces change, but as a leader, you will consistently be responsible for people. If you care about the people you lead, you have found a sustaining joy.

Effective caring can be quite difficult. We all care differently. We all demonstrate care in various ways. There is no universal, tried-and-true formula for success. The book *1001 Ways to Recognize Employees* taught me how to demonstrate caring in a few specific ways. I learned when I should recognize people and how to be more spontaneous about this recognition. I also learned tools like personal notes to employees and unannounced awards for achievements. The book taught me how to translate caring into something my employees could see. Yet the book did little to reinforce exactly how I care for the people I led.

Caring is more about how you feel. That means if you care about others naturally, you may have an easy time caring for the people you lead, like Buddy Rogers. However, if caring for others is not your strong suit, you must focus intentionally on caring. You must understand how to find compassion within your heart and figure out how to demonstrate that compassion effectively. Effective demonstration of caring is just as important as caring itself. You cannot underestimate the importance of how you show you care.

If, like me, caring is a weakness for you, you may need to build thoughtful caring into your schedule. I made a calendar entry once a week to write personal notes and had my staff bring me recommendations for recognition at subsequent staff meetings. The calendar reminder didn't change how I cared but changed how people saw that I cared. If you struggle in the same way, seek structure as a help.

If your issue is deeper, If you do not routinely feel for your employees, then structure is not your answer. There is only one route for you and that is prayer and perhaps counseling. If with God's help you cannot find a pathway to caring, then you should not be leading people. In fact, you should examine your salvation and read Paul's letters again. Christians are to clothe ourselves with compassion, wear it on the outside for all to see. Caring for others is a part of the mature Christian's lifestyle. If you are a Christian leader, you should model caring, which is important for your witness and vital to your joy.

Ask yourself these questions:

- Do I struggle to show I care, or do I have a deeper issue with caring?
- Am I close enough to God that caring shows in my countenance, in my daily walk?
- Do others see how much I care?

Today, pray for caring.

Pray that the Holy Spirit will shower your soul with compassion for others. Pray Colossians 3:12 that your heart might reflect that God dearly loves you. Confess your shortfalls and pray for improvement. Pray for compassion in your leaders, pray for your followers to hold you accountable and call you to action. Pray God will present you with an opportunity to demonstrate caring for your employees. Pray that God will strengthen your commitment to Him so that you might find deep compassion within your heart. Finally, thank God for your opportunities and praise Him for His leadership in your life.

DAY TWENTY-SEVEN
Imperative Three: Find Joy in All You Do

COURAGE

"Courage is the mental or moral strength to venture, persevere, and withstand danger, fear, or difficulty."[57]

Biblical Reference: Psalm 56:3-4 (NIV)

"When I am afraid, I will trust in you. In God, whose word I praise, in God I trust; I will not be afraid. What can mortal man do to me?"

This was a simple project, relocating a 25,000-volt (or 25 kV) overhead line from one side of the road to the other, making room for the new interstate. The crew worked diligently, and I was meeting with a telephone company representative on top of a nearby hill to measure clearances above the ground and between my power lines and his telephone lines. From our vantage point, we could see the entire job, about six poles that supported the power lines. The crew was finishing up pulling new wire, getting ready to attach it to the new poles they set across the road. They used a chain hoist to remove slack in the new wire, positioning wire for transfer from the pulleys to new insulators already in place on new wooden cross arms installed atop the new poles. The wire sat de-energized in the pulleys

---

[57] https://www.merriam-webster.com/dictionary/courage

waiting for when the crew was ready. The chain hoist capably absorbed slack on one side, while on the other side of the hoist, the wire was dipping lower and lower.

As the new bare aluminum wire dipped lower, the new wire inadvertently touched the nearby old wire, energized at 25 kV. Instantly, all the new wire "came hot" as line workers say. The new un-insulated wire was just sitting in pulleys. That means 25,000 volts just found a great pathway to ground, through the pulleys and into the six power poles where the pulleys sat. Immediately, all six poles caught fire on top, each with a nice blue plasma ball of an electrical fault. Each of the six poles had its own electrical roar, and the sound was impressive. While poles are a pretty good insulator, they are still an attractive pathway to ground. There was enough energy flow through the poles to make a spectacular scene, but not enough to trip off the energized line. The line just sat and burned as the telephone guy and I watched from the crest of the hill.

Honestly, the display of power was beautiful. Electric plasma balls have a distinctive color and sound. Couple that with orange flames and black smoke and we saw a cornucopia of sound and color. We stood for a moment without a word. I figured the line would soon burn through and break in half, dropping and extinguishing the arc. I was willing to wait. But as luck would have it, a school bus came over the hill just by us and stopped right below one of the burning poles and wire. The bus driver threw out his red, school-bus stop sign, a signal that he was ready to let off kids. The bus was sitting in a terrible spot, *right* under a newly energized wire, *right* under a fire. Plus, I knew at any moment the wire would break somewhere and come down, still energized at 25,000 volts. I was stuck. All this was going through my head, but I didn't know what to do. Even if I did, I couldn't make myself move at all.

I watched as the line workers jumped into action. The ground man was running toward the bus, under the burning lines, which were about to fall. He was warning the kids to stay on the bus. Up in the air, at the site of the chain hoist, the line worker in a bucket truck had a wrench and was swinging into the super-hot, blue plasma ball, trying to dislodge where the old wire had welded to the new wire in the intense heat. His only protection? His 25 kV rated rubber gloves. At that very moment the fault current finally reached a protection threshold and the line automatically de-energized.

All was silent, even as tendrils of smoke drifted from all six poles. The kids got off the bus without ever knowing their precarious situation.

I often thought about the actions of those two men. Talk about courage. Both moved instantly without concern for their own safety. I was dumbstruck standing on the hill watching while they acted. They moved with experience and practice. They had seen many electrical faults like this one. They had likely dealt with similar faults successfully in the past. When the time came, they acted automatically without considering the risks. Their actions were courageous, but also a practiced response.

Perhaps you will never have to swing a wrench into a hot ball of plasma, but you may have to stand firm before a hot boss, defending an employee or a peer. You may find yourself putting your own career at risk to save another. You may find yourself the lone holdout as you defend a right action. Leadership courage is about doing the right thing at the right time and feeling joy as you do so.

Courage as a leader most often translates into stepping into situations without the confidence or confirmation that all will be well. As many throughout history have stated, courage is not the absence of fear. Nelson Mandela, who demonstrated courage over and over again as he successfully fostered racial reconciliation in South Africa, was heard to say: "I learned that courage was not the absence of fear, but the triumph over it. The brave man is not he who does not feel afraid, but he who conquers that fear."[58]

Elisabeth Elliot served as a missionary to Ecuador in the mid-1900s. Even after the death of her husband at the hands of the Waorani tribe, she continued her dedicated service. She served two years as a missionary to the very tribe of people who murdered her husband. Elisabeth Elliot was a courageous woman. She often said courage was defined by those that chose to push ahead despite their fear.[59]

Courage is a sense, a feeling, an urge to push forward when the mind argues otherwise. What distinguishes the soldier who charges into danger from the soldier who hides away? Courage. For men and women

---

[58] https://www.independent.co.uk/news/world/nelson-mandela-10-inspirational-quotes-to-live-your-life-by-8988290.html

[59] https://www.goodreads.com/author/quotes/6264.Elisabeth_Elliot

on the front lines of danger, courage is often a spontaneous action born of training and experience. It may seem strange, but spontaneous courage takes practice. This is why soldiers train and train. They practice courage so when the time comes, courage is automatic. This automatic courage is also important in leadership positions. For leaders, courage can make the difference between success and failure. Good leaders learn to make courage look spontaneous, but this is a skill born of practice, knowledge, and heart. Good leaders learn to do it afraid as Elisabeth Elliot suggests. Leadership takes a practiced, measured approach. You train for courage, just like you train for any other skill you wish to master.

It is easy enough to see how the military can practice maneuvers, or how fire-fighters practice first response, but how can leaders practice courage? The training begins by watching others and seeing how they demonstrate courage in their actions. Find courageous leaders and take note of how they interact when faced with challenges. Like everything else, it is also helpful if you have an in-depth knowledge of the circumstances and a clear understanding of exactly what is happening. Moving forward with courage means you have assessed the risk and determined that it is worthy to move ahead.

But how can you assess the risk, absorb the knowledge, and still be spontaneous? Start with small, less risky decisions and ask yourself, "Am I being courageous or conservative?" Maybe even more importantly, ask if it is a time for courage or a time for a more measured response? As you practice, you get more accustomed to acting quickly, even automatically. For those watching you, this begins to look a lot like courage.

As a Christian you know and love the Bible. Bible training should be an enjoyable part of your life. And Bible training *is* courage training. Nowhere else can you find example after example of men and women who fought through their fears to do the right thing and experienced joy for doing so. Think of Joshua and Caleb defending entrance into the Promised Land as all the other spies warned of the danger. Joshua's joy was deferred for forty years before he led his people into the Promised Land.

Think of David, a shepherd boy who overcame the nine-foot tall, Philistine giant Goliath. David openly shared the joy of his relationship with the Lord as he danced freely before the people.

Think of Jesus as He set His face toward Jerusalem, knowing fully what awaited Him there. Jesus found joy in the fulfillment of His Father's plan, redeeming sinners and opening the doors to heaven. Jesus knowingly embraced the cross and stood down His earthly fear. Jesus was the most courageous person to ever walk the earth. If courage begins by watching and learning from those who are courageous, is there a better example than Jesus? You don't have to conquer your fears, just put them in perspective. As David writes in Psalm 56, "*What can mortal man do to me?* "

When you face difficulties, pray for the right response. Instead of praying for God to remove the fear, pray for God to give you the strength to stand strong despite the fear. It is a source of great joy to successfully stand firm and persevere despite fear.

Ask yourself these questions:

- Do I ever stand up for a person or principle, even when I am putting my reputation at risk?
- Are there courageous leaders in my life I can emulate?
- Do I use the Bible for training in courage?

Today, pray for courage.

Pray that the Holy Spirit will help you train for courage. Pray Psalm 56 that you might be able to put fear in perspective and trust in God. Confess your shortfalls and pray for improvement. Pray for your leaders to be courageous, pray for your followers to demonstrate courage. Pray God will present you with an opportunity to demonstrate your courage. Pray that God will strengthen your resolve to use the Bible as your training tool. Finally, thank God for your opportunities and praise Him for His leadership in your life.

DAY TWENTY-EIGHT
Imperative Three: Find Joy in All You Do

HUMILITY

> *"Humility is the feeling or attitude that you have no special importance that makes you better than others; lack of pride."*[60]

Biblical Reference: James 4:10

> *"Humble yourselves before the Lord and he will exalt you."*

My father died when he was sixty-three. My mom, my sister, and I watched him take his last breath. His year-long battle with cancer finally ended. The chemotherapy that made him so sick was over. The radiation experiment that left him unable to heal from the smallest wound was over. The surgeries were over —and also the weeks of recovery with no healing, leaving him weaker and weaker. So was the pain from the open surgical wound, which never healed because of the radiation. The inability to swallow food, the constant thirst, the never-ending weakness was all over. So too was the quick wit. Never again the impossible ingenuity that created things like a Chevy Vega truck and hearse camper. Never again

---

[60] https://dictionary.cambridge.org/us/dictionary/english/humility

the unspoken love that was so evident in the words and actions he shared with all of us. Never again. Cancer won. Death won.

Death is the ultimate lesson in humility. From dust we come and to dust we return. The greatest athlete is cut from the team as his skills evaporate. The greatest leader steps aside for new blood. Being the greatest means nothing. We are here for a moment in time. How can we not see our own humility? As individuals we are but a small drop in a very large sea.

It sounds hopeless. It sounds futile, doesn't it? It is. Death is the penultimate curse upon mankind. As humans, we cannot overcome death, we cannot defeat death. Yet there is hope. All throughout the Holy Bible reverberates the phrase *But God*. Death should win, *but God* has other ideas.

God has given us the gift of this life that we may live life abundantly. Our lives impact thousands, even millions of other lives. We are all linked together in this journey. When we consider the time we have, the joy we feel doing His work, how could we be anything but our best? How can we afford to hate, for example, when we could treat other people well? And how can we fail to lead well, when God provides us the tools and opportunities to lead? The influence we have over our family, our friends, our community explodes beyond our own vision to truly reflect the glory of God. After all, He made us in His image, to reflect His glory.

I often think back to special times with my dad. His hobby, really his side business, was restoring wrecked vehicles and selling them. We spent hours and hours together on those cars. I remember straightening bent frames by chaining cars to the big oak out front and jerking the other side with a tractor as hard as we could. He would site his eye down the frame and give it a thumbs up. We beat smashed parts back into life. We applied putty, "bondo" they call it, filling holes and cracks. And we sanded and sanded and sanded until we could not sand any more. Our victory lap was always painting. I applied tape to the car to ready it for painting, covering the windows, chrome, lights, and so forth. Taping is a meticulous job, a slow job, but a rewarding job. Pulling away the tape after the finished coat of paint displayed the culmination of weeks of work in a finished car.

Some days we kept a running conversation, but many days we just worked side-by-side, no words, just confirmation of this or that part of our work. Really, the quiet times are my favorite memories because that was who my dad was. He spoke without speaking. He was a special man who taught me during those long hours the importance of patience, of meticulous attention to detail, and the value of staying with a project until it was complete. Those lessons served me throughout my life. In the end, it was painting cars that led to his cancer. The toxic fumes inhaled over decades eventually brought forth the lung cancer and took his life.

But cancer doesn't win.

Death doesn't win.

God wins.

Yes, we lose battles, but victory waits for those who believe, like my dad. They stand ready to welcome those of us still at work here in this life. For our God is our Magnificent Father. He has prepared for our shortfalls. He understands the challenges of living life as humans. He beams with pride as we overcome our struggles. He celebrates our victories and mourns our defeats. When He looks at us, He should see our failures, our sin, our shortcomings. Instead God has placed Jesus in our life so the Lord might see beyond us to Jesus. Jesus covers our failures in His blood. Jesus covers our sins, our shortcomings through the power of the cross. There through His sacrifice and resurrection He not only defeated sin but defeated death itself.

God sees no shortfalls. No failures. When the Lord sees us, He sees the cleansing power of Jesus. We are as the unblemished lamb. Perfect in every way. Death *is* a defeated foe. How can that not bring us joy?

Christian leadership demands a humble perspective. Our understanding that *today* is but a fleeting moment thins our belief in our own abilities. Be humble, and He will exalt you. We are here to be the best we can. When our best is great, we can thank God for making it so. Just as when our best isn't good enough, God is there to listen and help.

Ask yourself these questions:

- Do I know how to be both confident and humble?
- Do I give credit to others or seek it for myself?
- Does my pride sometimes outshine my humility?

Today, pray for humility.

Pray that the Holy Spirit will keep you humble in all successes. Pray James 4:10 that you might remain humble before the Lord and your followers. Confess your shortfalls and pray for improvement. Pray for humility in your leaders, pray for your followers to accept your humility as a strength, not a weakness. Pray God will present you with an opportunity to demonstrate humility. Pray that God will strengthen your faith so that you might grow in humility. Finally, thank God for your opportunities and praise Him for His leadership in your life.

DAY TWENTY-NINE
Imperative Three: Find Joy in All You Do

MEEKNESS

"Meekness is the virtue whose purview is the governance of anger and related emotions."[61]

Biblical Reference: Matthew 5:5

"Blessed are the gentle, for they shall inherent the earth."

My mother, Nancy Gurkin Manning, comes from an interesting family. The Gurkin family has tempers. All seven brothers and sisters grew up with those tempers served regularly. Yet within them lurked another unexpected attribute, control. This control led to what the Bible calls meekness.

My grandfather, Jimmy Gurkin, was all Gurkin, temper included. He was a powerful man, a rough man with no filter. But Grandma, Mary Belle Gurkin, grew to become one of the sweetest women one would ever meet. She not only tolerated my grandfather's temper; she helped her children throttle their anger and turn it to passion and energy. Her example led the next generation of Gurkins, my mother and her siblings, to channel their anger toward the good things of life. She taught them to divert negative

---

[61] https://www.theatlantic.com/health/archive/2012/11/bringing-back-meekness-as-a-virtue/265009/

energy toward constructive accomplishments. The family didn't know the behavior they were learning would be what we think of today as biblical meekness. In other words, power under the control of the Holy Spirit.

The result of Jimmy's passion coupled with Mary Belle's control led to an amazing group of siblings. A group of men and women who never worked harder or cared more for each other. There was still anger, and plenty of it, but there was always an undercurrent of love and respect for one another. These siblings understood the powerful temper that hid within each of them. They allowed it to play out in their siblings. And they let the anger dissipate before working to slowly reel it back. Each one understood fiery tempers because each had their own. Anger did damage, as anger always does, but there was a great willingness to forgive and overcome the damage within the family.

My mother leveraged this foundation into a remarkable marriage. She became the stabilizing influence in our family. My dad could be a little reckless with money, infinitely creative, and unusually impetuous. Somehow my mom leveraged these tendencies to our advantage as a family, while tamping back his more impetuous personality with quiet authority. I realize now, looking back, she was teaching us biblical meekness. I still feel the inherited Gurkin family temper lurking deep within my own life, and it still comes out to visit from time to time. But I learned to control it most of the time through the example my mother set.

My mother restrained her own power to allow room for us all to thrive. I saw this in my parent's marriage all the time. One of my favorite memories happened along Route A1A in Florida. Our family had hit the road in my father's latest creation, that hearse camper. This was an early version, not much space. Basically, he welded a Mustang top to the hearse and cut a hole in the roof. Everywhere we went heads turned.

One early evening, we found ourselves parked in the Marine Land parking lot after hours. We always found free places to park. I remember my mom on her knees in the blue shag carpet of the hearse, cooking hamburgers on a propane grill about six inches off the floor. One window barely open, and that Florida kind of rain roaring outside on both the hearse and the Mustang roof. We were lucky not to die of carbon monoxide poisoning. This could have been a time for anger, for frustration, for exasperation, trapped in a weird creation of my dad's in the stifling humidity of a Florida evening. But my mom turned this into a time of joy, laughing at the absurdity of our circumstances. She was controlling her power, releasing her passion in little bits of love for her husband and her two children, sitting in a tin can stuck in a driving rain. And happy as could be. Those were the best hamburgers I ever ate.

I doubt you would find anyone who would say my mother is meek. She is smart, powerful, and articulate. She normally gets her way. Every once in a while—not much, but occasionally—that Gurkin temper rises to the surface. But most of the time, she is a picture of power under the control of the Holy Spirit. Her Gurkin heritage gifts her with remarkable energy. The energy that sometimes family members throttled toward anger, my mother manages to direct toward more positive emotions.

All her life, she has been a picture of Colossians 2:23, *"Whatever you do, work heartily, as for the Lord and not for men."* My mother worked any job. She worked every job. She kept the house functioning through difficult financial times. All the while my sister and I never realized we didn't have money. After many menial jobs, Nancy Gurkin Manning landed a wonderful opportunity as a certified purchasing agent at a mill in Washington, North Carolina. She even passed the certification tests as a licensed professional. Unfortunately, this happened at the same time my dad got cancer. Without hesitation, my mother resigned this dream job to be home with my dad. Later in her life, she painted houses with her sister—two sisters painting houses in their late seventies. Even now in her eighties, she volunteers to clean out people's attics to get prizes for the church yard sale. There is no doubt where I get my desire to always be working on some project.

My mother exemplifies power under control. Within her is a great energy longing to explode. Yet because of her relationship with God and years of self-training, she pushes that power to work, to love, and to support others. The Bible calls that meekness, power under control.

Meekness is not an attribute valued in leaders. When we think of *meekness*, we think it is only a couple letters away from *weakness*. We all know meek, quiet people, and we don't consider those people as leaders. So why is meekness an attribute of leadership? Think of Jesus first. In

Matthew 11:29, Jesus says, *"Take my yoke upon you, and learn from me, for I am gentle and lowly in heart, and you will find rest for your souls."*

We certainly don't think of Jesus as weak! Jesus has such great power, yet He calls Himself gentle and lowly in heart. Jesus leads through gentleness and caring. He is bold when He needs to be, yet quiet and listens, when appropriate. The meekness of Jesus reminds me of my mother. Overall, you would never call Jesus a meek man, yet He is a meek man. Meekness is a wellspring of amazing power, throttled effectively by the Holy Spirit. This power stands ready for us to use in positive endeavors at the command of those who gain mastery of this tremendous advantage.

Peter also highlights the gentle in spirit in 1 Peter 3:4 **"but let it be the hidden person of the heart, with the imperishable quality of a gentle and quiet spirit, which is precious in the sight of God."** Note Peter calls the imperishable quality of a gentle and quiet spirit the *"hidden person of the heart."* This is your true self, stripping away the anger. This is the person God wants you to be, to count you precious in His sight. Meekness is about allowing things to happen around you without taking over. Essentially, being easy and light, pushing down negative thoughts that you might overpower them.

What about you? Do you have control over your anger, your power? Do you harvest your power into positive energy? This is a remarkable attribute for a leader. Do you restrain your power to allow others to thrive? Rather than always controlling the circumstances, let the circumstances have a little more control of you. This attitude allows you to turn challenging situations to situations of joy. Which emotion do you believe people wish to see in their leader, anger or joy? Embrace meekness. After all, Jesus says I am meek and lowly.

And Jesus is the best leader of all time.

Ask yourself these questions:

- Do I ever feel out of control?
- Do I think of meekness as weakness?
- Can I learn to emulate Jesus in His powerful meekness?

Today, pray for meekness.

Pray that the Holy Spirit will give you power in control. Pray Matthew 5:5 that you might be among the blessed, who are gentle and will inherit the earth. Confess your shortfalls and pray for improvement. Pray for meekness in your leaders, pray for your followers to accept meekness as a strength, not a weakness. Pray God will present you with an opportunity to demonstrate power under control. Pray that God will strengthen your faith so that you might grow in meekness. Finally, thank God for your opportunities and praise Him for His leadership in your life.

DAY THIRTY
Time to SOAR.

Mount Up on Wings as Eagles!

Biblical Reference: Psalm 37:5-6

> *"Commit your way to the LORD; trust in him and he will act. He will bring forth your righteousness as the light, and your justice as the noonday."*

Lema Caranqui Aurelio is my Christian brother in Ecuador. Everyone knows him as Pastor Aurelio. My wife and I first meet Pastor Aurelio about five years ago. We were working to help establish One Heart Global Ministries in Ecuador with a new, One Heart missionary partner, Katty Aguirre. Katty arranged for our small mission team to visit Pastor Aurelio in Cebadas, Ecuador. Cebadas is a small community about an hour up the Andes mountains from Riobamba. There in Cebadas, Pastor Aurelio had a vision for a church. We went and passed rocks for the foundation. We mixed concrete on the ground and tied rebar for the walls. Together we began to form a foundation. This was the beginnings of a beautiful little church, but little did we know Pastor Aurelio had so much more in mind.

One year later we returned to the small church in Cebadas. Waiting there as we entered was everyone from the church family, celebrating our return. We worshipped with them and officially dedicated the new building. Then Pastor Aurelio began to share his true vision. He saw all of Ecuador blessed out of that little church. He saw community after community coming to Christ, each with a need for an anchor church, his church there in Cebadas. He saw a coliseum, a radio station, a bus service, a women's pregnancy center, and so much more. We did not know what to think of this man in Cebadas.

Five years later, Pastor Aurelio finished his coliseum in Cebadas. A giant structure, about the size of a football field with brick walls, a new metal roof, and a dirt floor. The coliseum may have a dirt floor, but it is *huge*. There in that coliseum, over thirty communities now come to worship once a month. You don't notice the dirt floor for the hundreds of worshippers. By the way, the Pregnancy Center of Cebadas is now open for business. The bus service and radio station remain in God's hands for the moment.

Our missionary, Katty, calls Pastor Aurelio the Apostle Paul of Ecuador. He works all day as a nurse in Riobamba, then visits new communities in the evening, spreading the word with his wife everyone calls Sister Clemencia.

Everyone loves Pastor Aurelio. Everyone recognizes him as a great Christian leader. But what people don't see is the price Pastor Aurelio pays for his leadership. Pastor Aurelio is Quichua. The Quichua people are indigenous to Ecuador, and over the years continued to move up into the high elevations of the Andes. There they became more and more isolated, more and more distant from the mainstream. Years ago, they would tell you they were Catholic. Over years of isolation, their Catholicism merged with traditional beliefs rooted in the Incan dynasty. Their theology today is a strange mixture of beliefs.

One such belief is that evangelical Christians are evil. Community leaders teach that Christian missionaries will *eat* their children. They teach that if they listen to Christian missionaries their crops will fail, their families will get sick and die. Their leaders teach that God will abandon them and their family. Pastor Aurelio walks into the villages of the Quichua, knowing he faces many of these beliefs.

Over and over Pastor Aurelio tells of persecution as he and Sister Clemencia enter new villages. Leaders threaten to tie them to trees and beat them. Their car is vandalized. Their children are ostracized, robbed, beaten up, ignored. Their lives threatened. Yet Pastor Aurelio stands fast, finding one or two families to visit in each community. He shares the gospel and gives that area to God. The word spreads quickly.

Often early believers also find persecution. Their power cut off. Their water cut off. Some lose their jobs. Yet, the gospel is stronger than their persecution, and they persevere. In time, the faithful look to build a small church, a place to gather. Katty begins to bring in medical and dental mission teams from the United States. Soon construction and evangelical teams join, and in time, the village becomes a beacon for Christ. By this time Pastor Aurelio has moved down the road to the next village where he follows the same process. He sees the same results. In five years, he has seen thirty-two new churches born in the mountains of Ecuador!

Pastor Aurelio is a Christian leader. By any measure, he is highly successful. He consistently does the right thing, even against threats on his life and the life of his wife. He studies the word. He seeks greater understanding that he might always know the right thing. And despite great persecution, he always shows the joy of a man walking in step with Jesus.

Yet in his day-to-day job, he is just another nurse. The hospital does not call him out for his great leadership skills, though he demonstrates them over and again on the mission field. The doctors recognize the joy in his life, but his joy does not lead to promotions or new assignments. Pastor Aurelio is simply Nurse Aurelio, a dedicated and thoughtful servant.

As you consider your role as Christian leader, think about Pastor Aurelio. Maybe your leadership role centers around the secular world, or maybe you are at the point of the evangelical spear, like Pastor Aurelio. As a Christian seeking an opportunity to lead, find your opportunities where God places them in your life. Find your satisfaction where God places you, where God uses you.

King David is one of the godliest leaders to ever live. Yet he sometimes struggled with how God used his leadership ability. In his later years, he reflected on a life of injustice that seemed to prevail no matter what he did. He loved King Saul, yet King Saul repeatedly attempted to kill him. He loved his sons, yet his oldest son, Absalom, captured David's throne, leaving him to flee for his life. All his life he sought to build the Lord's temple, yet God would pass that responsibility along to his son, Solomon. Despite the perceived injustice in David's life, he wrote Psalm 37 as a beautiful reflection of God's sovereign power over evil and injustice. Read the whole Psalm and you get the perspective that God's people will prevail, always and forever.

Psalm 37 is a victory song for Christian leaders. Here we see God's promise: no matter the battle, He will prevail. In my days of secular leadership, I often returned to verses five and six.[62] David writes when we trust in the Lord, it is the Lord who will act, not us. He will bring forth our righteousness. Read that carefully. It is not you or me who will act but *He* will act. There are thirty attributes in this book. No one can remember them all. We can never hope to internalize all that is necessary to be the Christian leader we hope to be. How can we remember if we want to be bold or be calm? How can we remember if we want to be passionate or patient?

Yet there is a secret way to full recall. There is a secret way to ensure you know exactly what to do when the time comes. The secret is right there in Psalm 37. Trust in the Lord, and He will bring forth your righteousness. After all, because of Jesus Christ, you have the righteousness of God as His gift to you. It is not necessary that you know and understand every possibility and potential. Top Tier Leadership is about letting God help you lead. There is no one higher than God. He alone stands on the top tier. And that same on-high God will bring to the surface that which you most need when you most need it, turning on your righteousness. The Lord will honor your work, but hard work is involved. Being a leader is difficult, challenging work. Being a leader requires devotion and dedication. Being a leader requires trust and perseverance, study and contemplation. The good news is God will honor your hard work and position you so the choices you make and the actions you take might glorify Him.

The key to successful leadership is trust. Trust in the Lord. Trust in hard work and preparation. Then trust yourself to internalize key leader attributes so they become instinctive as the Holy Spirit guides you. Over time, you will not need to remember to show passion and energy at the right time. You will not have to recall confidence and boldness. As you practice, these attributes become a part of how you lead. Allow your experience and knowledge to complement your natural goodness that

---

[62] Psalm 37:5-6, *Commit your way to the Lord; trust in him, and he will act. He will bring forth your righteousness as the light, and your justice as the noonday.*

comes from following Christ. Count on God (and preparation) to bring the right attribute to the right circumstance. Prepare—and then lead by instinct. Become a top-tier leader.

Think of it this way. You aren't doing anything special to be a Christian leader. You are simply fulfilling your direction to live like Christ. Just as Paul beautifully wrote to live is Christ, we are to live our lives more like Christ each day. As you lead, you are living your life as you should, day in and day out, as you emulate Jesus. When you model your life and your actions after Jesus, you model a victorious life, no matter the circumstances. You are living the life of victory even when life doesn't seem victorious. You may lead as a vice president at your company, or you may lead like Pastor Aurelio in the kingdom of God. Count either as victory.

Yet even the best of us need a central theme to reverberate in our heads so we stay on track. I can never remember all these attributes, so I stick with the big three imperatives:

Do the right thing.

Know the right thing to do.

Find joy in all you do.

This isn't my philosophy; I modeled these imperatives after our Savior's life.

Many times, in the ministry of Jesus, we see Him *doing the right thing* when others would have done something different. He called out Zacchaeus— the chief Jewish tax collector in Jericho whom the Jews hated because he worked for the Roman government—and had dinner in Zacchaeus's home. He challenged the Pharisees as others cowered. He healed the ones no one else noticed, like the woman with the issue of blood outside the home of Jairus, or the beggar on the steps of the temple. He even welcomed the repentant thief on the cross to paradise. Jesus saw people when others did not and took decisive action.

He also knew *the right thing to do* at all times. He could have known this instinctively as He is God, but instead He chose to work hard. He practically lived in the synagogue and over and over again demonstrated His knowledge of the Scriptures and prophecy. He did the hard work necessary to know what was right.

And *He found joy in all He did*. Even in His sacrifice the joy of Christ was evident as He asked Mary, *"Woman, why are you weeping?"*[63] As Hebrews 12:2 says, *"fixing our eyes on Jesus, the author and perfecter of faith, who for the joy set before Him endured the cross."* This is the joy He promises you as He spoke in John 15:11, *"These things I have spoken to you so that my joy may be in you, and that your joy may be made full."* Christian leaders claim this promise.

Focus on the hard work needed to fully understand what the right thing is. You might think of that as working heartily for the Lord. Then stand up and do the right thing. When times are hard, stand firm. When you face opposition, listen harder. Opposition shouldn't result in a shouting match. Instead think of opposition as a listening match. Search for ways to bring people to your side when you know the right thing to do. No matter the outcome, find your joy in the result. This will become your greatest witness: to find your joy, and then show your joy to the world.

You don't have to stand by the water cooler with a sign around your neck that says Christian leader. You don't have to quote the Bible in open meetings. You don't have to challenge other religions or other lifestyles. There may come a time in your life when shouting the gospel on the corner is your calling. Or maybe your calling is bringing the gospel to the Quichua in Ecuador, like Pastor Aurelio. Maybe your calling is to stay right where you are and be the best Christian leader you can be right where you stand. Think of it this way, just be a good person. A Christ-like person. A saved person, led by the Holy Spirit, and willing to listen and follow as the Spirit leads. Do the right thing. Know the right thing to do. Find joy in all you do and share your joy broadly. People will flock to your side. You will have more opportunities to lead and share the Lord than you could imagine when you simply live as He lived. I love the way Oswald Chambers describes living a Christ-like life: *"The most wonderful secret of living a holy life does not lie in imitating Jesus, but in letting the perfect qualities of Jesus exhibit themselves in my human flesh."*[64]

Finally, always remember these two words: *But God*. You may have an idea how you want your life to turn out, *but God* may have a different idea. You may plot your course and hold fast, *but God* may steer you in another

---

[63] John 20:15
[64] https://www.thespiritlife.net/facets/spirit/75-process/process-reflection/1386-july-23-devotional-oswald-chambers

direction along the way. You may find yourself living life differently than you once thought, but if you live in the will of God, find your joy there, mount up, and live your life soaring like an eagle.

As we began with Isaiah 4:28-31,[65] it is fitting we end there. It is my great hope that you renew your strength each day. That you run and not grow weary. That you walk and not faint. May you truly find a way to soar as the eagle in your leadership. May you be a light in the darkness, a beacon on the many, seemingly insurmountable hills in our world.

Please let me pray for you as we close our time together:

Father, thank you for this person before you as he or she holds this book right now. Thank you for your leadership in each life. Thank you, Lord, that you are greater than all of us, Thank you, Lord, that you have a plan for all of us. Thank you that you created us in your image so we might reflect you here on this earth.

Lord, I pray for the readers of this book, that you might fill their lives with the Holy Spirit and guide their steps. I pray that you might elevate their trust in you. I pray that you might bring forth your righteousness as a light in each life. No matter the circumstances, Lord, work in each life to bring out the best in each person so that he or she may soar to new heights of Christian leadership.

Thank you for your power that lives within us. Thank you for the opportunity to be a light in a dark world. Open our eyes that we may see opportunities as you place them before us. May we be worthy of the challenge set before us. Thank you for Jesus that we may come before you through His grace, by His sacrifice. Thank you, Lord, for answered prayer. May your Christian leaders become Christian warriors and change the world for your glory.

Amen.

---

[65] Isaiah 4:28-31: *"They who wait for the Lord shall renew their strength; they shall mount up with wings like eagles; they shall run and not be weary; they shall walk and not faint."*

Acknowledgements

I decided to write a book with around ten years remaining in my full-time, working career. From that moment I began to write down stories as they happen. I discovered by writing these stories down that a consistent theme began to emerge. No matter the story, there always seemed to be a reflection of God in each resolution. When I finally retired from the Electric Power Research Institute in 2018, I prayed for days about what I should write. My intentions all along were to write a standard leadership book, using stories to augment the three imperatives and the twenty-seven attributes. Then came the *"But God"* moment. No matter how much I tried to make stories fit with attributes, instead they kept pointing me to Scripture.

One morning I was reading a devotion book and it struck me, I was supposed to write a devotion book, not a book on secular leadership. God led me down this pathway for over a year until it became apparent there just was too much for a devotion book alone. As I wrote about my experiences, and my observations of the experiences of others, I began to feel God pointing me forward toward what became *Top Tier Leadership*. For me, this feeling was a clear confirmation of God's will for the book. Therefore, my most important acknowledgement is for God's leadership and guidance. Both in my writing, and in my life.

Yet many others also made this work possible. First and foremost, my editor extraordinaire, Janet Thoma. Janet's insights and guidance turned thirty disjointed stories into the single journey that is *Top Tier Leadership*. Several friends also contributed a great deal. Cheryl Smith, a Vice President with Wells Fargo Bank, pre-read the first draft and helped shape the final product. Karen Forsten, a leader with the Electric Power Research Institute, also read the first draft and despite facing a crisis of her own provided tremendous support and encouragement for me. Nancy McDowell, a long-time friend and advisor, who can find things others cannot. Thanks to Bill King for letting me use his picture of the construction team on the cover. My sister, Joy Holster, an editor and English teacher for years, offered fantastic advice, both professionally and personally. My daughter, Caroline Manning for lending her artistic abilities and meticulous attention to detail. Of course, my mom and dad started me on the pathway of leadership from the very beginning and I owe them more than I could every repay. And my wife, Susan, served to inspire me and encourage me over and over again. She also reviewed my first cut and final review, steering me toward both better theology and better English. It was her inspiration and creativity that led to the title *Top Tier Leadership*, not just a reference to top-notch leadership, but a play on words with the top tiers of the barn. I would never even have started this book without her there to encourage me.

Maybe I owe the most to the thousands of people I worked with over fifty years. Thanks to my tobacco family, Aunt Loreta and Uncle Zack and the gang. Thanks to the men and women in this book whose real names are unknown. And to those who allowed me to use their real names. To Bob and Clayton at TVA, who along with the rest of my TVA leadership team showed me how leadership and Christian leadership were one and the same. To Tom Kilgore, an extraordinary man and a great CEO. To Bill Johnson, the very model of leadership, a good friend and an amazing CEO. To my long-term friend and mentor, Benny McPeak, who always demonstrated how real leaders had to break from the pack from time to time. And finally, to one of my favorite people, and best of friends, Buddy Rogers. Buddy is a special leader and a special man who leaves his imprint on everything he touches.

Writing a story which is essentially a reflection of my life caused me to recognize the powerful influence we have on each other. The people in my life shifted the course of my life many times. Looking back, I can see how God uses everyone to accomplish His purpose, and I sincerely hope God will use this book to help you accomplish yours.

For more information, visit https://fb.me/toptierleadership

CPSIA information can be obtained
at www.ICGtesting.com
Printed in the USA
LVHW112217030820
662331LV00012B/130